SIMPLY PHOTOSHOP® ELEMENTS 8

by Mike Wooldridge

WILEY

First published under the title Teach Yourself VISUALLY Photoshop® Elements 8 by **Wiley Publishing, Inc.,** 10475 Crosspoint Boulevard, Indianapolis, IN 46256, USA

Copyright © 2010 by Wiley Publishing, Inc., Indianapolis, Indiana

This edition first published 2010.

Copyright © 2010 for the EMEA adaptation: John Wiley & Sons, Ltd.

Registered office

John Wiley & Sons Ltd, The Atrium, Southern Gate, Chichester, West Sussex, PO19 8SQ, United Kingdom

For details of our global editorial offices, for customer services and for information about how to apply for permission to reuse the copyright material in this book please see our website at www.wiley.com.

Permissions

Brianna Stuart http://www.stuartphotography.net Product screenshots reprinted with permission from Microsoft Corporation.

ISBN: 978-0-470-71128-6

A catalogue record for this book is available from the British Library.

Printed in Italy by Printer Trento

Publisher's Acknowledgements

Some of the people who helped bring this book to market include the following:

Editorial and Production

VP Consumer and Technology Publishing Director: Michelle Leete

Associate Director – Book Content Management: Martin Tribe

Associate Publisher: Chris Webb

Executive Commissioning Editor: Birgit Gruber

Publishing Assistant: Ellie Scott

Project Editor: Juliet Booker

Development Editor: Shena Deuchars

Marketing

Senior Marketing Manager: Louise Breinholt

Marketing Executives: Chloe Tunnicliffe and Kate Parrett

Composition Services

Layout: Amy Hassos, Andrea Hornberger, Jennifer Mayberry

Graphics: Jill Proll

Indexer: Potomac Indexing, LLC

Series Designer: Patrick Cunningham

About the Author

Mike Wooldridge is a Web developer in the San Francisco Bay area. He has authored more than 20 books for the Visual series.

Author's Acknowledgements

Mike thanks Brianna Stuart for the use of her beautiful photographs in some examples and for her help in preparing the hundreds of screenshots for the book. He thanks Christopher Stolle for his top-notch project editing, Dennis Cohen for his knowledgeable technical editing, Kim Heusel for his careful copy editing, and Ronda David-Burroughs, Cheryl Grubbs, and Mark Pinto for all their clever illustrations. This book is dedicated to Mike's wife Linda and son Griffin.

How to Use This Book

Do you look at the pictures in a book or newspaper before anything else on a page? Would you rather see an image instead of read about how to do something? Search no further. This book is for you. Opening *SIMPLY Photoshop Elements 8* allows you to read less and learn more about Photoshop Elements 8.

Who Needs This Book

This book is for readers who have never used image-editing software and want to learn how to work with digital photos on their computers. It is also for more computer-literate individuals who want to expand their knowledge of the different features that Photoshop Elements 8 has to offer.

What You Need to Use This Book

To install and run Photoshop Elements 8, you need a computer with the following:

- An Intel or compatible processor running at 2 GHz or faster
- Microsoft Windows XP with Service Pack 2 or 3, Windows Vista or Windows 7
- Colour monitor with a 1024x768 or greater resolution
- 1GB of RAM
- 1.5GB of available hard-drive space

You may find the following useful for capturing digital photos to use in Elements:

- Digital camera
- Image scanner
- Digital camcorder

The program's Web features require an Internet connection and a Web browser. The following browsers are supported:

- Microsoft Internet Explorer 6, 7 and 8; Firefox 1.5, 2 and 3; and Safari 2.0

The Conventions in This Book

A number of typographic and layout styles have been used throughout Simply Photoshop Elements 8 to distinguish different types of information.

Bold

Bold type represents the names of commands and options that you interact with. Bold type also indicates text and numbers that you must type into a dialog box.

Italics

Italic words introduce a new term, which is then defined.

Numbered Steps

You must perform the instructions in numbered steps in order to successfully complete a section and achieve the final results.

Bulleted Steps

These steps point out various optional features. You do not have to perform these steps; they simply give additional information about a feature.

Indented Text

Indented text tells you what the program does in response to your following a numbered step. For example, if you click a certain menu command, a dialog box may open or a window may open. Indented text may also tell you what the final result is when you follow a set of numbered steps.

Notes

Notes give additional information. They may describe special conditions that may occur during an operation. They may warn you of a situation that you want to avoid – for example, the loss of data. A note may also cross-reference a related area of the book. A cross-reference may guide you to another chapter or to another section within the current chapter.

Icons and Buttons

Icons and buttons are graphical representations within the text. They show you exactly what you need to click to perform a step.

You can easily identify the tips in any section by looking for the tip icon. Tips offer additional information, including hints, warnings and tricks. You can use the tip information to go beyond what you have learned in the steps.

Operating System Differences

The screenshots used in this book were captured using the Windows Vista operating system. The features shown in the tasks may differ slightly if you are using Windows 7, Windows XP or an earlier operating system. For example, the default folder for saving photos in Windows Vista is named "Pictures," whereas the default folder in Windows XP for saving photos is named "My Pictures." The program workspace may also look different based on your monitor resolution setting and your program preferences.

Table of Contents

1 GETTING STARTED

2 ORGANISING YOUR PHOTOS 22

3 IMAGE-EDITING BASICS 48

4 SELECTION TECHNIQUES 64

5 LAYER BASICS 86

CONTENTS

GETTING STARTED

Are you interested in working with digital images on your computer? This chapter introduces you to Adobe Photoshop Elements 8, a popular software application for editing and creating digital images.

Photoshop Elements lets you save your images in different file formats for use on the Web and in other applications. You can also share your photos by e-mailing them, putting them in an online gallery or printing them. For safekeeping, you can export your photos or back them up.

START PHOTOSHOP ELEMENTS

Photoshop Elements is a popular photo-editing program you can use to modify, optimise and organise digital images. You can use the program's Editor to make imperfect snapshots clearer and more colourful as well as retouch and restore older photos. You can also use the program's Organizer to group your photos into albums, assign descriptive keyword tags and create slide shows, online galleries and more.

1 Click **Start**.

2 Type **Elements** in the search box.

Windows displays a list of search results.

3 Click **Adobe Photoshop Elements 8.0**.

The Photoshop Elements welcome screen opens.

4 Click **Edit**.

The Photoshop Elements Editor opens.

A *You can click **Organize** to open the Organizer.*

B *You can also log in to or sign up for Adobe's photo-sharing and backup services.*

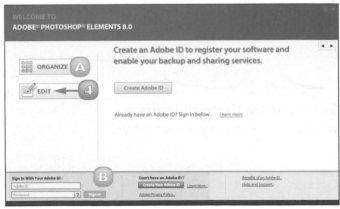

THE EDITOR WORKSPACE

In the Photoshop Elements Editor, you can use a combination of tools, menu commands and panel-based features to open and edit your digital photos. The main Editor pane displays the photos that you are currently modifying. This section gives you a preview of the interface elements in the Editor.

A Image Window
Displays the photos you open in Photoshop Elements.

B Layout Button
Opens a menu that lets you select from a variety of image window arrangements.

C Image Tabs
Clickable tabs for switching between open images in the Editor.

D Photoshop.com Links
Clickable links for signing in to Photoshop.com to manage your photos online.

E Organizer Button
Switches to the Organizer interface, where you can catalogue your photos.

F Task Tabs
Clickable tabs for switching between workflows in the Editor.

G Panel Bin
A storage area for *panels*, which are the resizable windows that hold related commands, settings and other information.

H Project Bin
Enables you to open and work with multiple photos.

I Toolbox
Displays a variety of icons, each representing an image-editing tool.

J Options Bar
Displays controls that let you customise the selected tool in the Toolbox.

THE ORGANIZER WORKSPACE

In the Photoshop Elements Organizer, you can catalogue, view and sort your growing library of digital photos. The main Organizer pane shows miniature versions of the photos in your catalogue. This section gives you a preview of the interface elements in the Organizer.

A **Photo Browser**

Displays miniature versions, or *thumbnails*, of the photos in your catalogue.

B **Toolbar**

Displays buttons and other options for modifying and sorting photos in the Photo Browser.

C **Photoshop.com Links**

Clickable links for signing in to Photoshop.com to manage your photos online.

D **Display Menu**

Contains commands for switching to different views in the Organizer.

E **Task Tabs**

Clickable tabs for switching between workflows in the Organizer.

F **Panel Bin**

A storage area for *panels*, which are the resizable windows that hold related commands, settings and other information.

G **Tag Icon**

Shows which tags have been applied to a photo.

H **Status Bar**

Displays the name of the currently open catalogue, how many photos are in the catalogue and other summary information.

SWITCH BETWEEN THE EDITOR AND THE ORGANIZER

Photoshop Elements has two main views: the Editor and the Organizer. The Editor enables you to modify, combine and optimise your photos, while the Organizer lets you browse, sort, share and categorise photos in your collection. You can easily switch between the two views.

1 Start Photoshop Elements in the Editor view.

You can open and edit a photo in the Editor.

2 Click **Organizer**.

The Organizer appears.

A You can click **Fix** and then **Full Photo Edit** to return to the Editor.

B A lock icon (🔒) appears on any Organizer photos that are currently being edited in the Editor.

THE PHOTOSHOP ELEMENTS TOOLBOX

Photoshop Elements offers a variety of specialised tools that let you edit your image. Take some time to familiarise yourself with the Toolbox tools.

You can select tools by clicking buttons in the Toolbox.

A Move
Moves selected areas of an image.

B Zoom
Zooms your view of an image in or out.

C Hand
Shows unseen parts of a larger image.

D Eyedropper
Samples colour from an area of an image.

E Marquee
Selects pixels by drawing a box or ellipse around the area you want to edit.

F Lasso
Selects pixels by drawing a free-form shape around the area you want to edit.

G Magic Wand
Selects pixels of odd-shaped areas based on similar pixel colour.

H Quick Selection Brush
Selects pixels by using brush shapes.

I Type
Adds text to an image.

J Crop
Trims an image to create a new size.

K Cookie Cutter
Crops your image into shapes.

L Straighten
Straightens a tilted image.

(M) Red-Eye Removal
Corrects red-eye problems.

(N) Spot-Healing Brush
Quickly fixes slight imperfections by cloning nearby pixels.

(O) Clone Stamp
Duplicates an area of the image.

(P) Eraser
Erases pixels.

(Q) Brush
Paints strokes of colour.

(R) Smart Brush
Simultaneously selects objects and applies colour adjustments.

(S) Paint Bucket
Fills areas with colour.

(T) Gradient
Creates blended colour effects to use as fills.

(U) Custom Shape
Draws predefined shapes.

(V) Blur
Blurs objects in your image.

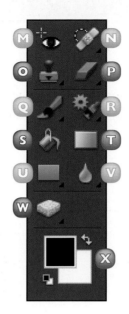

(W) Sponge
Adjusts colour saturation or intensity.

(X) Foreground and Background Colours
Sets foreground and background colours to use with tools.

WORK WITH TOOLBOX TOOLS

You can use the tools in the Photoshop Elements Toolbox to make changes to an image. After you click to select a tool, the Options bar displays controls for customising how the tool works. Some tools include a tiny triangle in the bottom-right corner to indicate hidden tools you can select. For example, the Marquee tool has two variations: Rectangular and Elliptical.

Select a Tool

1 Position the mouse pointer over a tool.

A *A screen tip displays the tool name and shortcut key. You can click the tool name to access Help information about the tool.*

2 Click a tool to select it.

B *The Options bar displays customising options for the selected tool.*

3 Specify any options you want for the tool.

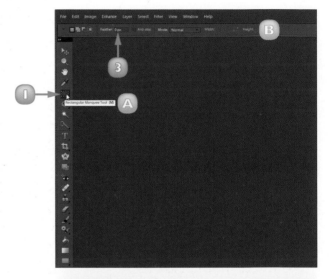

Select a Hidden Tool

1 Click a tool that has a triangle in its corner and hold the mouse button.

A *A menu of hidden tools appears.*

You can also right-click on a tool to show hidden tools.

2 Click the tool you want to use.

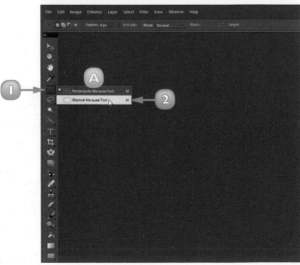

10

Configure the Toolbox

1 At the top of the Toolbox, click **⏵⏵**.

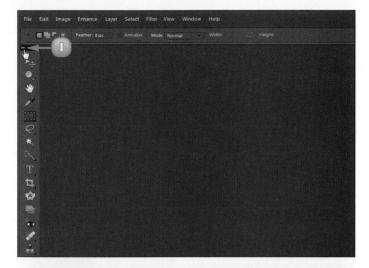

The Toolbox changes configuration.

In this example, the one-column Toolbox changes to a two-column Toolbox.

Ⓐ *You can click* **⏴⏴** *to switch back to the previous configuration.*

Both the one-column and two-column configurations are used in the examples in this book.

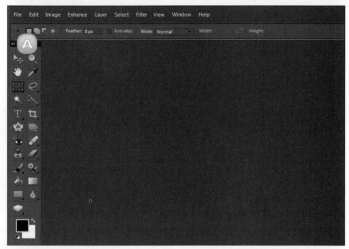

Float the Toolbox

1 Position the mouse over the top of the Toolbox.

2 Click and drag the Toolbox to a different part of the workspace.

3 Release the mouse button.

Photoshop Elements displays the Toolbox as a floating panel.

Note: *You can drag the Toolbox back to the left side of the workspace to unfloat it.*

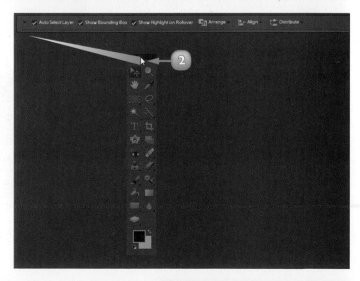

WORK WITH PANELS

In the Photoshop Elements Editor, you can open resizable windows called *panels* to access different Photoshop Elements commands and features. By default, most panels open in the Panel Bin located on the right side of the Photoshop Elements workspace. You can float panels over the program workspace to give yourself easy access to commands.

Open and Close a Panel

1 Open the Photoshop Elements Editor.

2 Click **Window**.

3 Click a panel name.

A check mark (☑) next to a panel name indicates the panel is already open.

The chosen panel opens.

Ⓐ You can hide or show a panel by double-clicking its title tab.

4 Click the panel menu.

A menu with panel commands opens.

5 Click **Close**.

The panel closes.

Float a Panel

① Click and drag the title tab of a panel to the work area.

② Release the mouse.

The panel opens as a free-floating window.

Ⓐ You can resize a floating panel by clicking and dragging its corner (■).

Ⓑ To close a floating panel, click the **Close** button (✕).

Ⓒ To reset the Photoshop Elements panels to their default arrangement, click **Reset Panels**.

Rearrange Panels in the Panel Bin

① Position the mouse over the title tab of a panel.

② Click and drag the panel to a different part of the Panel Bin.

Ⓐ Photoshop Elements highlights the area to which the panel will be moved.

③ Release the mouse button.

Photoshop Elements moves the panel.

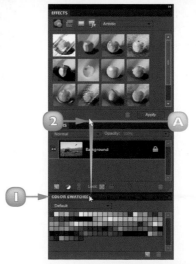

SET PROGRAM PREFERENCES

The Preferences dialog box lets you change default settings and modify how the program looks. You can set preferences in both the Editor and Organizer workspaces to customise the program to match how you like to work.

Editor Preferences

1 In the Editor, click **Edit**.

2 Click **Preferences**.

3 Click **General**.

The Preferences dialog box opens and displays the General options.

4 Select any settings you want to change.

A *You can specify the shortcut keys for stepping backward and forward through your commands.*

B *You can specify that images open in floating windows instead of tabbed windows.*

5 Click a different preference category.

C *You can also click **Prev** and **Next** to move back and forth between categories.*

In this example, the Preferences dialog box displays Units & Rulers options.

 You can specify the default units for various aspects of the program.

⑥ Click **OK**.

Photoshop Elements sets the preferences.

Organizer Preferences

① In the Organizer, click **Edit**, **Preferences** and then **General**.

The Preferences dialog box opens.

② Select any settings you want to change.

 You can specify date ordering and formatting preferences.

③ Click **OK** to close the dialog box.

Photoshop Elements sets the preferences.

 You should use measurement units applicable to the type of output you intend to produce. Pixel units are useful for Web imaging because monitor dimensions are measured in pixels. Inches, picas, centimetres and millimetres are useful for print output.

 The Editor Performance preferences show how much memory you have available and how much Photoshop Elements is using. You can change these settings to enhance the program's performance. Use the Scratch Disks preferences to allocate extra memory on your hard drive, called scratch disk space, to use if your computer runs out of RAM.

IMPORT PHOTOS FROM A DIGITAL CAMERA OR CARD READER

You can import photos into Photoshop Elements from a digital camera or directly from the camera's memory card. Most cameras and card readers manufactured today connect to a computer through a USB port. A typical PC comes with multiple USB ports. Make sure the device is properly connected before you begin. Some computers have special media slots that accept memory cards for transferring photos and other files.

Every camera and card reader works differently. Consult the documentation that came with your device for more information.

1 In the Organizer, click **File**.

2 Click **Get Photos and Videos**.

3 Click **From Camera or Card Reader**.

The Photo Downloader dialog box opens.

Note: *Photo Downloader may open automatically when you connect your device to your computer.*

4 Choose your camera or memory card from the Get Photos from menu.

By default, Photoshop Elements downloads your photos into dated subfolders inside your Pictures folder.

Ⓐ *You can click **Browse** to select a different download location.*

Ⓑ *You can click here to choose a different naming scheme for the subfolders.*

5 Choose a naming scheme for your files.

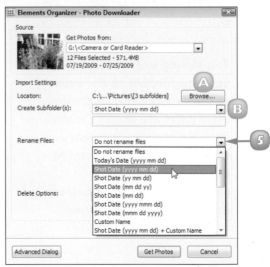

6 Choose whether to keep your photos on the device or delete them after downloading.

C *You can click this check box to use the current settings whenever a photo device is connected to your computer (☐ changes to ☑).*

7 Click **Get Photos**.

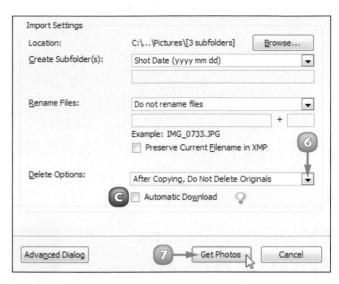

Photoshop Elements downloads the photos from the device.

After downloading the photos, Photoshop Elements adds them to the current Organizer catalogue. You can add the photos to albums and perform other functions.

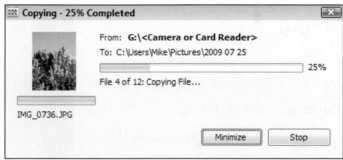

Use the Advanced Photo Downloader Dialog Box

1 Click **Advanced Dialog** in the bottom-left corner of the Photo Downloader.

2 Click the check box for each photo you want to import from your device (☐ changes to ☑).

3 Click this check box to turn on red-eye correction (☐ changes to ☑).

4 Type creator and copyright details to be applied to all the imported photos.

5 Click **Get Photos**.

IMPORT PHOTOS FROM A SCANNER

You can import a photo into Photoshop Elements through a scanner attached to your computer. You can scan black-and-white and colour photos. To scan an image, make sure the scanner is properly connected before you begin. Some scanners include slide or film attachments that enable you to also digitise slides or film.

Every scanner works differently. Consult the documentation that came with your scanner for more information.

1 In the Organizer, click **File**.

2 Click **Get Photos and Videos**.

3 Click **From Scanner**.

   The Get Photos from Scanner dialog box opens.

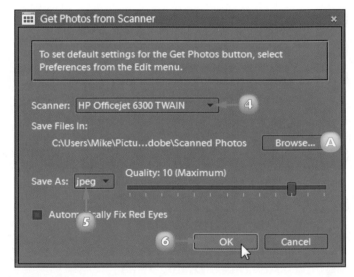

4 Click here to choose your scanner.

   Ⓐ *You can click **Browse** to choose a location other than the default folder.*

5 Click here to choose a file format.

6 Click **OK**.

   The software associated with your scanner opens.

7 Change your scanning settings as needed. You may need to specify whether the photo is black and white or colour. You may also get to preview the scan.

8 Click a button to scan the photo.

   The image is scanned and added to the current catalogue in the Organizer.

IMPORT PHOTOS FROM A FOLDER

You can use the Organizer program in Photoshop Elements to import images from a folder on your computer or a disc. You may find this useful if you already have an archive of digital photos on your PC or on photo CDs.

① In the Organizer, click **File**.

② Click **Get Photos and Videos**.

③ Click **From Files and Folders**.

The Get Photos from Files and Folders dialog box opens.

④ Click here to choose the folder containing your photos.

⑤ Hold Ctrl and click to select the photos you want to import. You can press Ctrl + A to select all the photos in the folder.

⑥ Click **Get Media**.

Photoshop Elements downloads the selected photos.

Search Computer for Photos

① Click **File**, **Get Photos and Videos** and then **By Searching**.

The Search dialog box opens.

② Click here to choose all hard drives, a single hard drive or a folder.

③ Click **Search**.

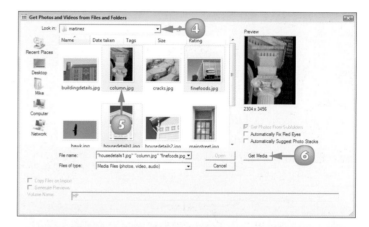

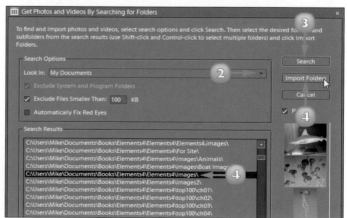

Photoshop Elements performs a search and displays a list of folders that contain photos.

④ Select one or more folders and then click **Import Folders** to get the photos. You can hold Ctrl and click to select multiple folders.

SAVE A PHOTO

You can save a photo in Photoshop Elements to store any changes that you made to it. PSD is the default file format for Photoshop Elements. Photoshop Elements supports a variety of other image file formats, including the popular JPEG, GIF, and PNG formats often found on the Web.

You can save multiple versions of the same image as a version set in the Organizer.

Save a New Photo

1 In the Editor, click **File**.

2 Click **Save As**.

Note: *For photos that you have previously saved, you can click **File** and then **Save**.*

The Save As dialog box opens.

3 Type a name for the file.

A *You can click here to choose another folder or drive in which to store the file.*

B *You can click here to choose another file format.*

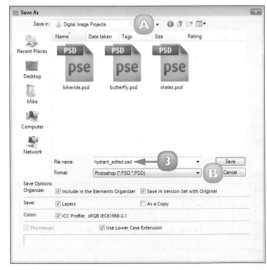

4 Click this check box to include the saved file in the Organizer (□ changes to ☑).

5 Click this check box to save the edited file with other versions of the same file in the Organizer (□ changes to ☑).

You can save a photo into a version set only when the photo already exists as a version in the Organizer.

6 Click **Save**.

Photoshop Elements saves the file.

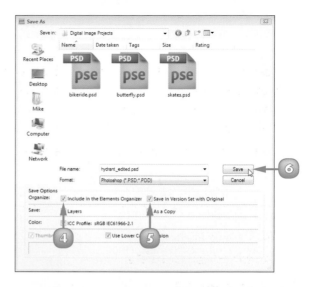

View a Version Set in the Organizer

1 In the Organizer, find a version set. Version sets have light grey boxes around them and are marked with a ▣ icon.

A *You can use the scrollbar to browse photos.*

2 Click here to expand (▶) the version set so you can view all the photos in that set.

Photoshop Elements expands the set.

Save Open Photos as an Album

1 In the Editor, open the photos you want to save as an album.

2 In the Project Bin, click **Bin Actions**.

3 Click **Save Bin as an Album**.

4 Type a name for the album.

5 Click **OK**.

The photos are saved as a new album in the Organizer.

CONTENTS

2

ORGANISING YOUR PHOTOS

Are you ready to organise your digital photos? You can catalogue, view and sort photo files using the Organizer. A complement to the Editor in Photoshop Elements, the Organizer helps you manage your growing library of digital pictures by categorising them in a variety of ways. This chapter shows you how to take advantage of the many photo-management features in the Organizer.

OPEN THE ORGANIZER

You can organise and manage your digital photos in the Organizer in Photoshop Elements. The Organizer works alongside the Editor to help you keep track of the digital photos and other media you store on your computer. You can open the Organizer from the welcome screen that appears when you first start up Photoshop Elements or you can switch to it from the Editor.

The Organizer offers basic editing commands under the Fix tab. The commands can save you from having to switch to the Editor to optimise your photos.

From the Welcome Screen

1 Start Photoshop Elements.

   The welcome screen appears.

2 Click **Organize** to open the Organizer.

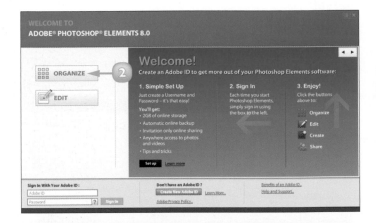

   The Organizer opens.

   To import photos into the Organizer workspace, see Chapter 1.

   To create a new catalogue with which to organise your photos, see the next section, "Create a Catalogue".

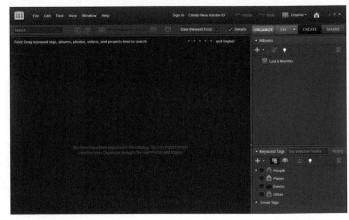

From the Editor

1. Start Photoshop Elements.

2. From the welcome screen that appears, click **Edit** to open the Editor.

3. Click **Organizer**.

The Organizer opens.

A You can return to the Editor by clicking **Fix** and then clicking **Full Photo Edit**.

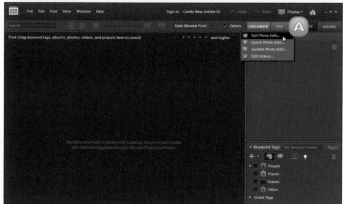

Edit Photos from Within the Organizer

1. In the Organizer, click **Fix**.

The editing buttons appear.

2. Click a thumbnail to select a photo to edit.

3. Click an Auto button to optimise the colour or lighting of your photo.

A You can click **Crop** to open an image for cropping (see Chapter 3).

CREATE A CATALOGUE

The photos you manage in the Organizer are stored in catalogues. You can keep your photos in one large catalogue or separate them into smaller catalogues. When you start the Organizer, Photoshop Elements creates a default catalogue for you, called My Catalog.

You can organise your photos within a catalogue into smaller groups called albums. See the section "Work with Albums" for more information.

① In the Organizer, click **File**.

② Click **Catalog**.

Ⓐ *You can restore a catalogue you have previously backed up by clicking **Restore Catalog from CD, DVD or Hard Drive**.*

The Catalog Manager dialog box opens.

Photoshop Elements lists the available catalogues.

③ Click **New**.

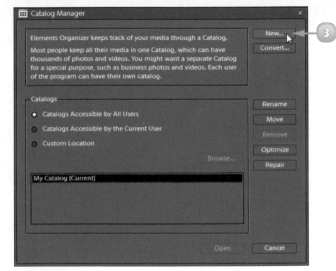

Type a name for the new catalogue.

 Click **OK**.

Photoshop Elements creates the new catalogue and opens it.

B *Photoshop Elements displays the name of the current catalogue.*

C *The number of files in the catalogue and the range of dates for the files are displayed here.*

Note: *To add photos to your catalogue, see Chapter 1.*

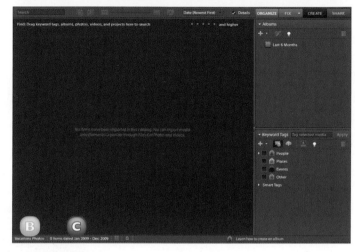

☑ **To switch to a different catalogue in the Organizer, open the Catalog Manager. Select the catalogue that you want to open in the catalogue list and then click Open. You can open only one catalogue at a time in the Organizer.**

☑ **You can edit a catalogue so that only the user who is currently logged in to your computer can access it. Open the Catalog Manager. From the list that appears, select the catalogue that you want to protect and then click Move. A dialog box opens to let you change the accessibility of the catalogue.**

VIEW PHOTOS IN THE MEDIA BROWSER

After you add photos to your catalogue, you can view them using the Organizer's Media Browser. The Media Browser displays thumbnails or miniature versions, of your photos, along with details about those photos. You can filter, sort and change the size of the thumbnails.

1 Open the Organizer.

The Media Browser displays the photos in the Organizer catalogue.

2 Click and drag the thumbnail size slider (■) to change the size of the thumbnails.

A *You can click ■ to maximise the thumbnails.*

B *You can click ■ to minimise the thumbnails.*

C *You can use the scrollbar to browse other thumbnails in the Media Browser.*

3 Click here and then click **Date (Oldest First)**.

The Media Browser displays the oldest photos at the top.

D *The star rating and date details appear below each photo.*

4 Click **Details** (☑ changes to ■).

Photoshop Elements hides the photo details.

 You can filter the file types that appear in the Media Browser. In the Organizer, click View. Click Media Types. Uncheck a media type. Photoshop Elements hides the media type in the Media Browser.

28

VIEW A PHOTO IN FULL SCREEN MODE

You can switch to Full Screen mode in the Organizer to get a clearer view of your photos. Photoshop Elements expands the photo to fill the workspace and displays special panels for applying commands.

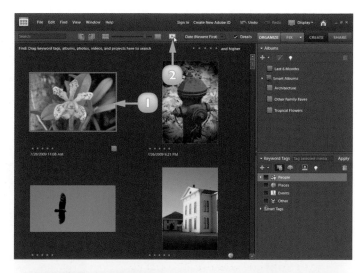

① In the Organizer, click the photo you want to view in Full Screen.

② Click 🖼.

Photoshop Elements opens the photo in Full Screen mode.

Ⓐ *The Quick Edit panel contains tools for editing images.*

Ⓑ *The Quick Organize panel contains tools for adding images to albums and applying keyword tags.*

Ⓒ *The panels automatically hide if not used. You can click Auto Hide (🔲) to turn hiding on and off.*

③ Click ➡ to go to the next photo in the Organizer. You can also press ➡.

Photoshop Elements displays the next photo.

④ Click ✖ or press Esc to exit Full Screen mode.

DISPLAY A SLIDE SHOW IN FULL SCREEN MODE

You can play a slide show in Full Screen mode to cycle through large versions of your images. You can choose background music and transition effects to accompany the slides.

1 Display the images you want to view as a slide show in the Media Browser.

A *You can click an album to display its photos as a slide show.*

2 Click ▣.

Photoshop Elements displays the first image in Full Screen mode.

3 Click the **Open Settings Dialog** button (🔧).

The Full Screen View Options dialog box opens.

4 Click here to choose background music.

B *You can click Browse to look for music on your computer to use as background music.*

5 Click **OK** to close the dialog box.

6 Click the **Transitions** button ().

The Select Transition dialog box opens.

7 Click a transition effect to display between slides in the slide show.

  C *You can roll your mouse over an option to preview an option.*

8 Click **OK** to close the dialog box.

9 Click the **Play** button (▶) or press Spacebar.

Photoshop plays the slide show, cycling through the images.

You can click the Play button again to pause the slide show.

Customise a Slide Show

1 Click **Open Settings Dialog** (🔧).

The Full Screen View Options dialog box opens.

  A *You can choose a slide duration here.*

  B *Click here to automatically start the slide show when you open Full Screen mode (■ changes to ✓).*

  C *Click here to display captions for photos that have them (■ changes to ✓).*

  D *Click here to play the slide show again when it finishes (■ changes to ✓).*

2 Click OK to save the settings.

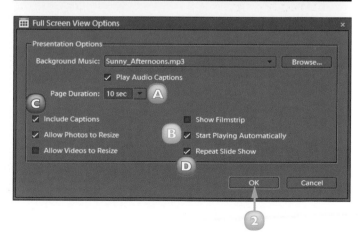

VIEW PHOTO PROPERTIES

You can view the properties for any photo in your catalogue. The Properties box displays a photo's general information, which includes the file name, file size, image size and location. You can also view any associated tags, file history and metadata information. Metadata, also known as EXIF data, is detailed information about how a digital photo was taken; it includes camera settings, such as exposure time and f-stop.

① In the Organizer, right-click on a photo.

② Click **Show Properties**.

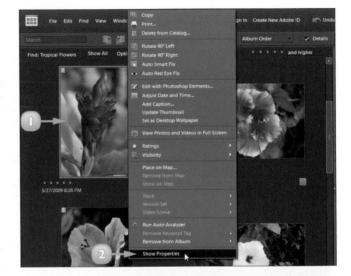

The Properties dialog box opens with the General properties shown.

(A) *You can add or edit a caption for the photo here.*

(B) *The rating, size, capture date and other information for the photo are shown here.*

③ Click the **Metadata** button (■).

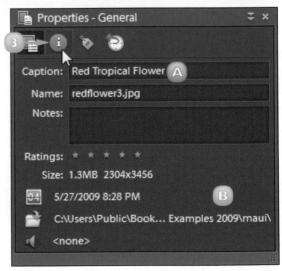

The Metadata properties appear. This includes the camera model and settings, if the photo came from a digital camera.

C *You can click here to display the complete metadata for a photo (● changes to ○).*

④ Click the **Keyword Tags** button (▣).

The Keyword Tags properties appear.

Photoshop Elements displays any keyword tags or albums associated with the photo. You can right-click on a tag or album to remove it from the photo.

D *You can click the **History** button (▣) to view Organizer statistics for the photo.*

⑤ Click ✕ to close the Properties dialog box.

Change a Photo's Date and Time

① Right-click on the photo you want to edit.

② Click **Adjust Date and Time**.

③ Click the **Change to a specified date and time** radio button (● changes to ○).

④ Click **OK**.

⑤ In the Set Date and Time dialog box, set the new date and time.

⑥ Click **OK**.

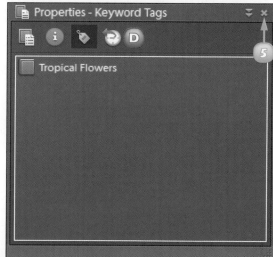

ADD A CAPTION

In the Organizer, you can add captions to your photos to help you remember important information about the images you catalogue. For example, you can add captions to your vacation pictures with details about the location or subject matter. Captions appear below a photo when the image is viewed in Single Photo View.

① In the Organizer, right-click on the photo you want to caption.

② Click **Add Caption**.

The Add Caption dialog box opens.

③ Type a caption for the photo.

④ Click **OK**.

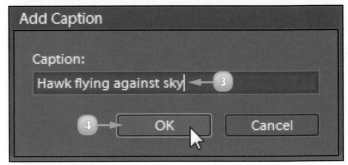

The Organizer adds the caption to the photo.

5 Click the **Single Photo View** button ().

A large thumbnail of the photo appears.

A *The caption appears below the photo.*

 You can also add captions to your photos by using the Properties box.

 To edit a caption, view the photo in Single Photo View in the Media Browser window. Click the caption and make your changes. You can delete the caption completely, type a new caption or make changes to the existing caption text. Press Enter to save your changes.

WORK WITH ALBUMS

Albums are a way to organise your photos within an Organizer catalogue. For example, you can take photos shot at a particular time or place and group them as an album. This makes it easier to find the photos later.

You can also organise photos in a catalogue using keyword tags. See the "Work with Keyword Tags" section later in this chapter for more information.

Create a New Album

1. In the Organizer, open the catalogue within which you want to create an album.

2. Open the Albums panel in the Panel Bin.

3. Click the plus sign (▪) and then click **New Album**.

The Album Details panel opens.

4. Type a name for the album.

   A. *You can assign the album to an album category.*

   B. *If logged in, you can click here to back up your album photos using the Photoshop.com service (▪ changes to ☑).*

5 Click and drag a photo from the Media Browser to the Items list.

The Organizer adds the photo to the album.

6 Repeat Step **5** for all the photos you want to add to the album.

You can hold **Ctrl** and click to select multiple photos and then click and drag to add them all to the album.

7 Click **Done** to close the Album Details panel.

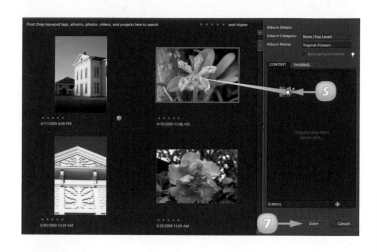

View an Album

1 Click the album name in the Albums panel.

The Organizer displays all the photos in the album.

A *Photos assigned to an album are marked with an Album icon.*

B *You can click **Show All** to return to the entire catalogue.*

C *You can click the trash icon (🗑) to delete the album.*

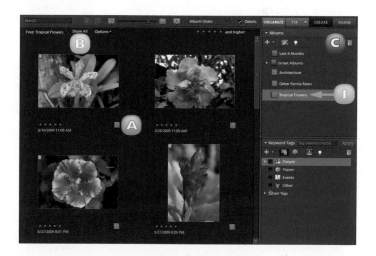

Remove a Photo

1 Under the photo in the Media Browser, right-click on the Album icon.

2 In the menu that appears, click **Remove from *Name* Album**.

The Organizer removes the photo from the album. The Album icon under the photo disappears.

VIEW PHOTOS BY DATE

To help you keep track of your photos, the Organizer can sort your images by date and display those that were taken during a specific date range. You can also view the images for a particular date range as a slide show.

1 In the Organizer, click **Display**.

2 Click **Date View**.

The Organizer displays a calendar view of your catalogue.

A *You can view your photos by year, month or day. In this example, the Month view is displayed.*

B *To see a different month, click the **Previous Month** (◉) or **Next Month** (◉) buttons.*

3 Click the date for the photos you want to view.

C *The first photo in the group appears here.*

4 Click the **Play** button (◉).

The Organizer starts a slide show, displaying each photo from the date you selected.

D *To pause or stop the sequence, click the **Pause** button (▣).*

To view the previous image, click the **Previous Item** button (▣).

To view the next image, click the **Next Item** button (▣).

⑤ Click the **Find in the Media Browser** button (▦).

The Media Browser appears with the photo from the Date View selected.

You can get to the Media Browser from the Date View by clicking **Display** and then **Media Browser**.

 *In the Media Browser, you can browse photos by date by clicking and dragging along a timeline. Click **Window**. Click **Timeline**. You can click and drag the endpoints to limit the range of dates.*

FIND PHOTOS

The Organizer offers a variety of methods for finding particular photos in your catalogue. You can search for photos by date, file name, tags, text and more.

In this section, you search for photos taken during a specific date range and with specific associated text.

Find Photos by Date

1 In the Organizer, click **Find**.

2 Click **Set Date Range**.

The Set Date Range dialog box opens.

3 Select the start date for the date range you want to search.

4 Select the end date for the date range you want to search.

5 Click **OK**.

The Organizer displays any matching photos in the Media Browser.

A *A summary appears at the bottom of the Media Browser.*

You can reset the date search by clicking **Find** and then **Clear Date Range**.

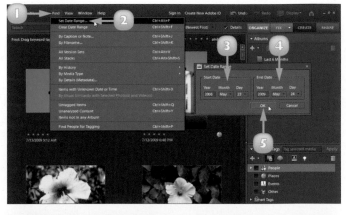

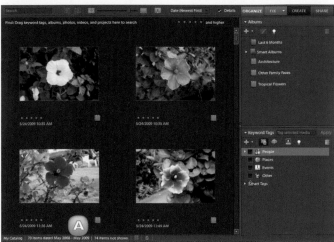

Find Photos by Text

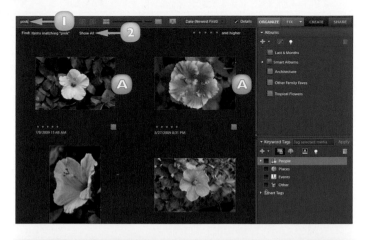

1 Type one or more keywords in the search box.

Photoshop Elements searches the file names, captions, keyword tags, album names and other text associated with your photos.

A *Photoshop Elements displays photos associated with the text as you type.*

If you type multiple keywords, photos must be associated with all the keywords to match.

2 Click **Show All**.

Photoshop Elements cancels the search and displays all the photos.

 You can access other ways to search from the Find menu. You can search by caption or note, filename, history or media type; for photos without a date or time; for photos with a visual similarity to selected photos and videos; for untagged items; and for items not in an album.

WORK WITH KEYWORD TAGS

Keyword tags help you categorise and filter your photos. You can assign the Organizer's preset tags or use tags that you have created. You can also assign more than one tag to a photo.

Preset tags include those for people, family, friends, places and events. You can assign tags to categories and subcategories.

Create a Keyword Tag

1 In the Organizer, open the **Keyword Tags** panel in the Organizer bin.

2 Click the plus sign (**+**) and then click **New Keyword Tag**.

The Create Keyword Tag dialog box opens.

3 Choose a category for the new tag.

4 Type a name for the keyword tag.

Ⓐ *You can add a note about the keyword tag here.*

5 Click **OK**.

Assign Tags

1 Click and drag a tag from the Keyword Tags panel to the photo that you want to tag.

Ⓐ *A keyword tag icon indicates that the photo has a tag assigned to it.*

Note: *You can also drag a thumbnail image from the Media Browser to a keyword tag.*

② To find an existing tag, type text in the Keyword Tags search box.

Photoshop Elements suggests tags with that text.

③ Click a tag in the list that appears.

④ Hold down **Ctrl** and click to select photos you want to tag.

⑤ Click **Apply**.

Photoshop Elements applies the tag to the selected photos.

Edit a Keyword Tag

① Right-click on the keyword tag and then choose **Edit *name* keyword tag**.

The Edit Keyword Tag dialog box opens.

② Type a new keyword tag name or make other edits to the tag.

③ Click **OK**.

Photoshop Elements applies the changes. Any images that have the keyword tag applied are updated.

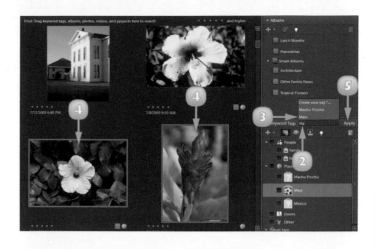

continued ➡

After you assign keyword tags, you can filter your catalogue to show only those photos that have certain tags. For example, you can filter your photos to show only photos of people or events. You can also simultaneously filter on multiple keyword tags.

You can view your keyword tags as a tag cloud, which organises tags alphabetically and sizes them by the number of times applied. You can click tags in the tag cloud to filter the photos in the Media Browser.

Filter By Tags

1. Open the Keyword Tags panel.

2. Click the box next to the keyword tag on which you want to filter (■ changes to ▦).

Note: *You can click* ▶ *to expand and* ▼ *to collapse a tag category.*

To filter by more than one keyword tag, you can click additional tags.

The Organizer displays the photos that share the selected keyword tags.

View a Tag Cloud

1. Open the Keyword Tags panel.

2. Click the **View Keyword Tag Cloud** button (▦).

   A. *A tag cloud displays the tags in alphabetical order and sized according to the number of times they are used.*

3. Click a keyword tag.

44

B *Photoshop Elements highlights the term.*

C *Only the photos tagged with that term are shown in the Media Browser.*

Only one tag in the tag cloud may be selected at a time.

4 Click the keyword tag again to remove the highlighting and reset the view in the Media Browser.

Remove a Tag from a Photo

1 Right-click the photo from which you want to remove a tag.

2 Click **Remove Keyword Tag**.

3 Click the keyword tag you want to remove.

The Organizer removes the keyword tag from the photo.

Export Keyword Tags

1 Open the Keyword Tags panel.

2 Click the plus sign ().

3 Click **Save Keyword Tag(s) to File**.

A *To import tags from a file, you can click From File.*

4 In the dialog box, click **Export All Keyword Tags** (● changes to O).

5 Click **OK**.

A Save dialog box opens, allowing you to save the keyword tags as an XML file.

> **The regular search box suggests keyword tags as you type search terms.**

CONTENTS

3

IMAGE-EDITING BASICS

Are you ready to start working with images? This chapter shows you how to fine-tune your workspace to best arrange your open images. You also discover how to change the on-screen image size, set a print size and change the print resolution.

MANAGE OPEN IMAGES

You can open a photo in the Editor to modify it or use it in a project. You can also open photos from the Organizer for editing in the Editor.

Each image you open in Photoshop Elements appears in its own window. Tabs at the top of the windows enable you to switch between images. You can also use the Project Bin or Window menu to view different open images.

Open a Photo

1. In the Editor, click **File**.

2. Click **Open**.

3. Navigate to the folder that contains the file you want to open.

4. Click the photo you want to open.

5. Click **Open**.

   Photoshop Elements opens the image.

Using Tabs

1. In the Editor, open two or more images.

   A. *Each open image has its own tab, which displays its file name and magnification.*

2. Click the tab for the image you want to view.

   The image appears as the active image.

Using the Project Bin

1. If the Project Bin is closed, you can click **Window** and then **Project Bin** to open it.

   A. *By default, the Project Bin displays smaller versions, or thumbnails, of the images.*

2. Double-click a thumbnail.

   The image appears as the active image.

Using the Window Menu

1. Click **Window**.

2. Click an image file name.

   The image appears as the active image.

   A. *You can click ☒ to close an image.*

continued →

You can view multiple images at the same time by choosing a layout. In Photoshop Elements 8, layouts allow you to display images as a grid, in vertical columns or in horizontal rows.

Using Layouts

① Click the layouts ▪.

Photoshop Elements displays a menu of layouts.

② Click a layout from the top row: one image at a time or multiple images in a grid, in vertical columns or in horizontal rows.

Photoshop Elements displays multiple windows — each with a different image.

③ Click the layouts ▪.

Ⓐ *The lower rows enable you to display a specific number of images at a time. A 3-Up layout displays three image windows.*

④ Click a layout.

50

Photoshop Elements displays multiple windows at once — each with a different image.

Note: *If you have more open images than windows, you can click tabs to switch between images.*

 When the Zoom tool (⬛) is selected, you can click the Zoom All Windows check box (⬛ changes to ☑) in the Options bar to make the tool affect all windows.

 The layout menu contains commands for controlling image windows. Click Match Location to view the same area in each open window. Click Match Zoom to view each open window at the same zoom percentage.

USE THE ZOOM TOOL

You can change the magnification of an image with the Zoom tool. This enables you to view small details in an image or view an image at full size.

You can move an image within the window using the Hand tool or scrollbars. The Hand tool helps you navigate to an exact area in the image by dragging freely in two dimensions.

Increase Magnification

1 In the Editor, click the **Zoom** tool (🔍).

2 Click the image.

Photoshop Elements increases the magnification of the image.

Ⓐ *You can select an exact magnification by typing a percentage value in the Options bar or in the lower-left corner of the image window.*

Decrease Magnification

1 Click the **Zoom Out** button (🔍).

2 Click the image.

Photoshop Elements decreases the magnification of the image.

Magnify a Detail

1. Click the **Zoom In** button (⊕).

2. Click and drag with the **Zoom** tool (🔍) to select a detail.

   The area appears enlarged on screen.

   The more you zoom in, the larger the pixels appear and the less you see of the image's content.

View at 100% Magnification

A. *Double-click the **Zoom** tool (🔍).*

B. *Click **1:1** on the Options bar.*

C. *Click **View** and then **Actual Pixels** from the menu.*

D. *Type **100%** in the Options bar field.*

E. *Type **100%** in the lower-left corner of the image window.*

F. *Right-click on the image and select **Actual Pixels**.*

G. *Press Alt + Ctrl + 0.*

Adjust the Image View

1. In the Editor, click the **Hand** tool (✋).

2. Click and drag inside the image window.

   The view of the image shifts inside the window.

   A. *You can also click and hold one of the window's scrollbar buttons (▲, ▼, ◄ or ►).*

CHANGE THE IMAGE SIZE

You can change the on-screen size of an image you are working with in Photoshop Elements to make it better fit the confines of your monitor. Shrinking an image can also lower its file size and make it easier to share via e-mail or on the Web.

When you change an image's on-screen size, you need to resample it. Resampling is the process of increasing or decreasing the number of pixels in an image.

① In the Editor, click **Image**.

② Click **Resize**.

③ Click **Image Size**.

The Image Size dialog box opens, listing the width and height of the image in pixels.

You can also press Alt + Ctrl + I to open the Image Size dialog box.

Ⓐ To resize by a certain percentage, click here and change the units to **percent**.

④ Click the **Resample Image** check box (■ changes to ☑).

Note: The Bicubic Smoother option is often better for enlarging, while the Bicubic Sharper option is better for shrinking.

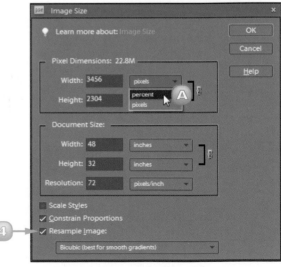

5 Type a size or percentage for a dimension.

> **B** *You can click the **Constrain Proportions** check box (■ changes to ☑) to cause the other dimension to change proportionally.*

6 Click **OK**.

> **C** *You can restore the original dialog box settings without exiting the dialog box by pressing and holding **Alt** and then clicking the **Cancel** button (which changes to Reset).*

Photoshop Elements resizes the image.

Note: *Changing the number of pixels in an image can add blur. To sharpen an image, see Chapter 6.*

Change the Image Print Size

> **A** *The Document Size section lists the current width and height of the printed image.*

1 Click here to change the unit of measurement.

> **B** *If you click the **Resample Image** check box, Photoshop Elements adjusts the number of pixels in the image. Otherwise, it adjusts the resolution.*

2 Type a size for a dimension.

3 Click the **Constrain Proportions** check box (■ changes to ☑) to cause the other dimension to change proportionally.

4 Click **OK**.

Photoshop Elements resizes the image.

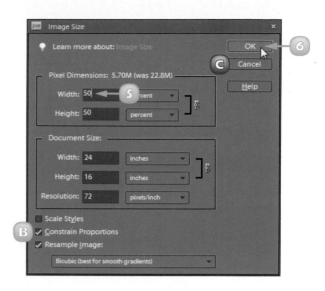

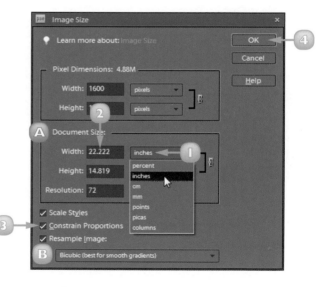

> ✓ **To preview an image's printed size, click File. Click Print to see the Print Preview dialog box. Click Print to print the image.**

CHANGE THE IMAGE RESOLUTION

You can change the print resolution of an image to increase or decrease the print quality. The resolution, combined with the number of pixels in an image, determines the size of a printed image. The greater the resolution, the better the image appears on the printed page – up to a limit, which varies with the type of printer you use and the paper on which you are printing.

1 In the Editor, click **Image**.

2 Click **Resize**.

3 Click **Image Size**.

The Image Size dialog box opens, listing the current resolution of the image.

A *You can click here to change the resolution units.*

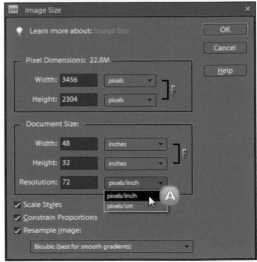

④ Type a new resolution.

Ⓑ *You can deselect the* **Resample Image** *check box (✔ changes to ■) to keep the number of pixels in your image fixed and change the printed dimensions. The print quality will change.*

⑤ Click **OK**.

Ⓒ *You can restore the original dialog box settings by pressing and holding* **Alt** *and clicking the* **Cancel** *button (which changes to Reset).*

Photoshop Elements adjusts the image resolution.

If you deselected the Resample Image check box, the number of pixels stays the same, as does the on-screen image size. Increasing the resolution makes the print size smaller and decreasing the resolution makes it bigger.

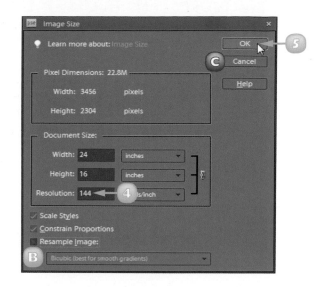

 To determine the printed size of a Photoshop Elements image, you can divide the on-screen size by the resolution. If you have an image with an on-screen width of 480 pixels and a resolution of 120 pixels per inch, the printed width is 4 inches.

 For most standard inkjet printers, a resolution of 300 pixels per inch should be sufficient to produce good-quality prints on photo-quality paper. A resolution of 150 pixels per inch is sufficient for regular copier paper. Printing at lower resolutions may cause elements in your image to appear jagged.

CHANGE THE IMAGE CANVAS SIZE

You can alter the canvas size of an image to change its rectangular shape or add space around its borders. The canvas is the area on which an image sits. Changing the canvas size is one way to crop an image or add *matting*, which is blank space, around an image.

58

① In the Editor, click **Image**.

② Click **Resize**.

③ Click **Canvas Size**.

The Canvas Size dialog box opens, listing the current dimensions of the canvas.

Ⓐ *You can click here to change the unit of measurement.*

Ⓑ *You can click here to specify the matte colour, which appears when you enlarge a dimension of your image.*

Ⓒ *You can click here or select **Other** to select a custom colour.*

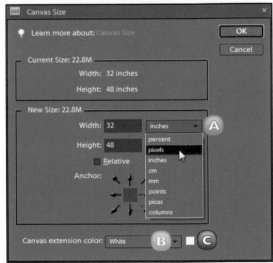

④ Type the new canvas dimensions.

　Ⓓ *You can click an arrow (▧) to determine in which directions Photoshop Elements changes the canvas size. Clicking the square in the middle of the arrows changes it equally on all sides.*

⑤ Click **OK**.

Note: *If you decrease a dimension, Photoshop Elements displays a dialog box asking whether you want to proceed.*

Photoshop Elements changes the image's canvas size.

In this example, because the width is increased, Photoshop Elements creates new canvas space on the sides of the image.

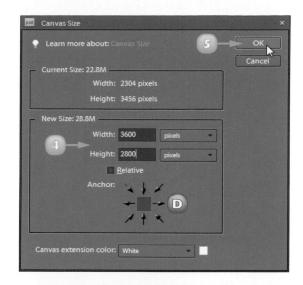

CROP AN IMAGE

You can use the Crop tool to quickly remove the top, bottom or sides of an image. Cropping is a great way to edit out unwanted background elements or reposition a subject in your photo.

You can also crop an image by reducing its canvas size (see the section "Change the Image Canvas Size"). Another way to crop is by selecting an area with a selection tool, clicking **Image** and then clicking **Crop**. See Chapter 4 for more on making selections.

---

1. In the Editor, click the **Crop** tool (▣).

2. Click and drag to select the area of the image you want to keep.

   A *You can set specific dimensions for a crop by using the Width and Height boxes in the Options bar.*

3. Click and drag the side and corner handles (□) to adjust the size of the cropping boundary.

   You can click and drag inside the cropping boundary to move it without adjusting its size.

4. Click ✓ or press **Enter** to accept the crop.

You can also double-click inside the crop area to crop the photo.

B *To exit the cropping process, you can click ⊘ or press* **Esc**.

Photoshop Elements crops the image, deleting the pixels outside the cropping boundary.

Note: *You can also crop images in the Quick Fix window. See the section "Quick Fix a Photo" in Chapter 6.*

Crop an Image into an Interesting Shape

1. Click the **Cookie Cutter** tool (⬠).

2. Click ▪.

3. Click a shape for the crop.

A *You can click here to access additional shapes.*

4. Adjust the cropping boundary and then perform the crop just as when using the regular Crop tool.

Photoshop Elements crops the image as a shape.

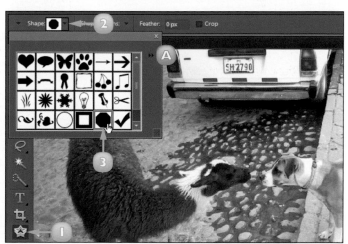

ROTATE AN IMAGE

You can use the rotate actions on an image to turn it within the image canvas. If you import or scan a horizontal image vertically, you can rotate it so that it appears in the correct orientation.

You can also flip a photo to change the direction of the subject matter. Flipping it horizontally, for example, creates a mirror image of the photo.

The Straighten Image command is useful for fixing photos that have been scanned crookedly.

Rotate 90 Degrees

1 In the Editor, click **Image**.

2 Click **Rotate**.

3 Click **90° Left** or **90° Right** to rotate the image.

A To change subject direction, click **Flip Horizontal** or **Flip Vertical**.

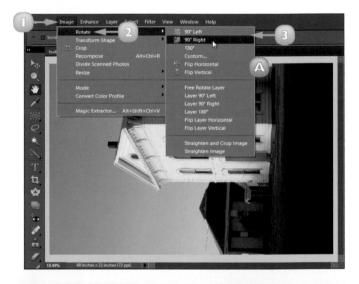

Photoshop Elements flips the image.

 You can rotate an image by a precise amount. Click Image, Rotate, Custom. In the Rotate Canvas dialog box, type an angle from -359.99 to 359.99. Click a direction to rotate. Click OK.

 If a photo has been scanned crookedly, click Image, Rotate, Straighten Image. You can click Straighten and Crop Image to crop any space that is left after straightening.

UNDO CHANGES TO AN IMAGE

You can undo commands by using the Undo History panel. This enables you to correct mistakes or change your mind about operations you have performed on your image. The Undo History panel lists recently executed commands, with the most recent command at the bottom.

You can also discard (or revert) all your changes.

1. In the Editor, click **Window**.

2. Click **Undo History**.

   The Undo History panel opens.

3. Click the **History** slider (■) and then drag it upward.

   Ⓐ You can also click a previous command in the Undo History panel.

Photoshop Elements undoes the previous commands.

   Ⓑ You can click and drag the slider down to redo the commands.

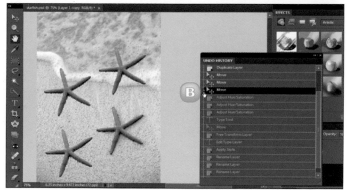

You can revert an image to the previously saved state and start over on the image editing. In the Editor, click Edit. Click Revert.

CONTENTS

4

SELECTION TECHNIQUES

Do you want to move, colour or transform parts of your image independently from the rest of the image? The first step is to make a selection. This chapter shows you how to use the Photoshop Elements selection tools to isolate portions of your images for editing and then manipulate them.

SELECT AN AREA WITH A MARQUEE

You can select parts of an image for editing by using a marquee. You can then make changes to the selected area using other Photoshop Elements commands.

Two marquee tools are available: the Rectangular Marquee enables you to select rectangular shapes, including squares and the Elliptical Marquee enables you to select elliptical shapes, including circles.

Select with the Rectangular Marquee

1. In the Editor, click the **Rectangular Marquee** tool ().

2. Click and drag diagonally inside the image window.

   You can press and hold Shift while you click and drag to create a square selection.

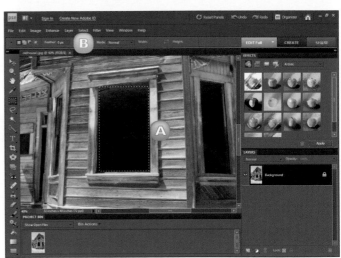

A *Photoshop Elements selects a rectangular portion of your image.*

You can reposition a selection by pressing the keyboard arrow keys: ⬆, ⬇, ⬅ and ➡.

B *You can deselect a selection by clicking **Select** and then **Deselect** or by clicking outside the selection area.*

Select with the Elliptical Marquee

① Right-click on the **Rectangular Marquee** tool (▦).

② Click the **Elliptical Marquee** tool (◉).

③ Click and drag diagonally inside the image window.

To create a circular selection, press and hold Shift while you click and drag. You can press and hold Shift + Alt to draw the circle directly out from the centre.

Ⓐ *Photoshop Elements selects an elliptical portion of your image.*

You can reposition selections by pressing the keyboard arrow keys: ↑, ↓, ← and →.

Note: *You can deselect a selection by clicking* **Select** *and then* **Deselect** *or by clicking outside the selection area.*

 You can customise the marquee tools (▦ and ◉) using the boxes and menus in the Options bar. A Feather value softens your selection edge – Photoshop Elements selects pixels near the edge by building a transition between the selection and the surrounding pixels. The Mode list enables you to fix the size or aspect ratio. You can type an exact width and height for a fixed-size selection or a ratio for a fixed-aspect selection.

SELECT AN AREA WITH A LASSO

You can create oddly shaped selections with the lasso tools. You can then make changes to the selected area using other Photoshop Elements commands. You can use three types of lasso tool: the regular Lasso, the Polygonal Lasso and the Magnetic Lasso.

You can use the regular Lasso tool to create freehand selections. The Polygonal Lasso tool lets you easily create a selection composed of many straight lines. The Magnetic Lasso tool automatically applies a selection border to edges as you drag. It works best when the element you are trying to select contrasts sharply with its background.

Select with the Regular Lasso

1 In the Editor, click the **Lasso** tool (🔗).

2 Click and drag with your mouse pointer (𝒫) to make a selection.

Ⓐ *To accurately trace a complicated edge, you can magnify that part of the image with the Zoom tool (🔍).*

3 Drag to the beginning point and then release the mouse button.

Photoshop Elements completes the selection.

 To select everything in your image, click Select and then click All. You can also press Ctrl+A on the keyboard. For multilayer images, Select All selects all the pixels in the currently selected layer.

Select with the Polygonal Lasso

1 Right-click on the **Lasso** tool ().

2 Click the **Polygonal Lasso** tool (📐).

3 Click multiple times along the border of the area you want to select.

4 To complete the selection, click the starting point or double-click anywhere in the image. Photoshop Elements adds a final straight line that connects to the starting point.

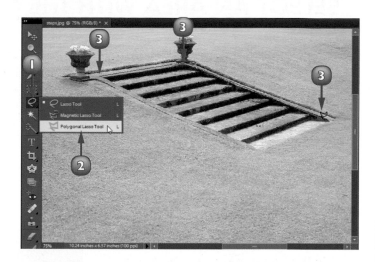

Select with the Magnetic Lasso

1 In the Editor, right-click on the **Lasso** tool (📐).

2 Click the **Magnetic Lasso** tool (📐).

3 Click the edge of the object you want to select to create a beginning anchor point, a fixed point on the lasso path.

4 Drag your mouse pointer (📐) along the edge of the object.

The path snaps to the edge of the element as you drag.

To help guide the lasso, you can click to add anchor points as you go along the path.

You can press Delete to remove the most recently added anchor point.

5 Click the beginning anchor point to finish your selection.

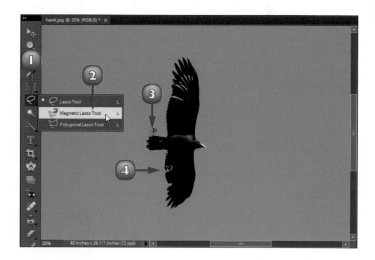

> *You can use the Options bar to adjust the Magnetic Lasso tool's precision. Width controls how many nearby pixels the lasso considers when creating a selection. Contrast controls how much contrast is required for the lasso to consider something an edge. Frequency controls how often anchor points appear.*

SELECT AN AREA WITH THE MAGIC WAND

You can select groups of similarly coloured pixels with the Magic Wand tool. You may find this useful if you want to remove an object from a background.

By specifying an appropriate tolerance value, you can control how similar a pixel needs to be for Photoshop Elements to select it.

① In the Editor, click the **Magic Wand** tool (🪄).

The mouse pointer (👆) changes to a magic wand (🪄).

② Type a number from 0 to 255 in the Tolerance field.

To select a narrow range of colours, type a small number; to select a wide range of colours, type a large number.

③ Click the area you want to select inside the image.

Ⓐ *Photoshop Elements selects the pixel you clicked plus any similarly coloured pixels near it.*

Ⓑ *To select all the similar pixels in the image, not just the contiguous pixels, deselect the* **Contiguous** *check box (☑ changes to ⬛). See the Tip for more.*

This example shows a greater number of similarly coloured pixels has been selected – all of the sky above the person.

C The tolerance value is greater.

④ To add to your selection, press Shift and then click elsewhere in the image.

Photoshop Elements adds to your selection.

D You can also click the selection buttons in the Options bar to grow or decrease the selection.

To ensure that the Magic Wand tool selects all instances of a colour in an image, deselect Contiguous (☑ changes to ■) on the Options bar.

SELECT AN AREA WITH THE QUICK SELECTION TOOL

You can paint selections onto your images by using the Quick Selection tool. The tool automatically expands the area you paint over to include similar colours and textures. This tool offers a quick way to select objects that have solid colours and well-defined edges.

You can adjust the brush size of the tool to fine-tune your selections.

① In the Editor, click the **Quick Selection** tool (▨).

② Click to open the Brush menu.

In the Brush menu, you can specify the tool's size and other characteristics. Decreasing the tool's hardness causes it to partially select pixels at the perimeter.

③ Click and drag inside the object you want to select.

A *Photoshop selects parts of the object based on its colouring and the contrast of its edges.*

B *After you make a selection, the Add to Selection button (■) becomes active.*

4 Click and drag to select more of the object.

C *Photoshop adds to the selection.*

Adjust the Selection

1 In the Options bar, click **Refine Edge**. The Refine Edge dialog opens.

A *You can increase **Smooth** to lessen the sharpness of any corners in your selection.*

B *You can increase **Feather** to make the edges of your selection partially transparent.*

C *You can use **Contract/Expand** to decrease or increase the selection slightly.*

D *You can define your selection with a custom overlay colour.*

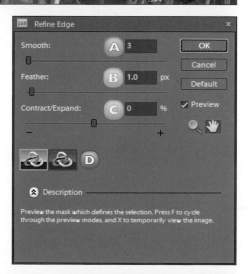

SELECT AN AREA WITH THE SELECTION BRUSH

You can select oddly shaped areas in your image by painting with the Selection Brush. By customising the size and hardness of the brush, you can accurately trace edges that are curved or not well-defined.

The Selection Brush differs from the Quick Selection tool in that it selects only the area you paint over and does not automatically select similar pixels. The Selection Brush's Mask option enables you to define the area that is not selected by using a partially transparent colour. It enables you to see the soft edges created by a soft selection brush.

Select with the Selection Brush

1. Right-click on the **Quick Selection** tool (▨).

2. In the Editor, click the **Selection Brush** tool (▨).

3. Click here.

   A slider (▥) appears.

4. Click and drag the slider to specify a size.

   You can also type a size.

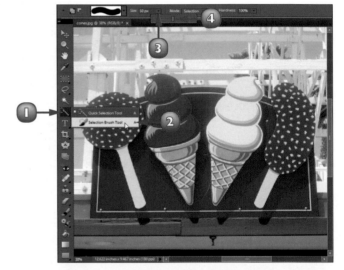

5. Type a hardness from 0% to 100%.

   A smaller value produces a softer selection edge.

6. Click the **Mode** drop-down arrow (▾) and then click **Selection**.

7. Click and drag to paint a selection.

8 Click and drag multiple times to paint a selection over the area you want to select.

Photoshop Elements creates a selection.

You can change the brush settings as you paint to select different types of edge in your object.

Deselect with the Selection Brush

1 Click the **Selection Brush** tool (■).

2 Click the **Subtract from Selection** button (■).

3 Click and drag where you want to remove the selection area.

Photoshop Elements removes the selection.

Paint a Mask

1 Click the **Mode** dropdown arrow (■) and then click **Mask**.

2 Click and drag to define the mask.

By default, the masked area appears as a see-through red colour, called a *rubylith*.

To turn it into a selection, click the **Mode** dropdown arrow (■) and then click **Selection**.

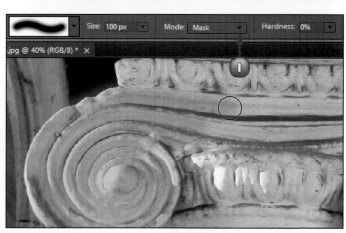

SAVE AND LOAD A SELECTION

You can save a selected area in your image to reuse later. This can be useful if you anticipate future edits to the same part of your image. You can load the saved selection instead of having to reselect it.

Save a Selection

1. In the Editor, use one of the selection tools to select part of the image.

2. Click **Select**.

3. Click **Save Selection**.

   The Save Selection dialog opens.

4. Make sure New is chosen in the Selection field.

5. Type a name for the selection.

6. Click **OK**.

   Photoshop Elements saves the selection.

Load a Selection

1. Click **Select**.

2. Click **Load Selection**.

   The Load Selection dialog opens.

3. Click here and choose the saved selection you want to load.

4. Click **OK**.

   The selection appears in the image.

INVERT AND DESELECT A SELECTION

You can invert a selection to deselect what is currently selected and select everything else. This is useful when you want to select the background around an object.

You can deselect a selection when you are done manipulating what is inside it or if you make a mistake and want to try selecting again.

Invert a Selection

1 In the Editor, use one of the selection tools to select part of the image.

2 Click **Select**.

3 Click **Inverse**.

A *Photoshop Elements inverts the selection; in this example, the bottom of the image is selected.*

Note: *You can also press* Shift + Ctrl + I *to invert the selection.*

Deselect a Selection

1 In the Editor, the selection tools have been used to select part of the image.

A *In this example, a small penguin is selected.*

2 Click **Select**.

3 Click **Deselect**.

Photoshop Elements deselects the selection.

Note: *You can also press* Ctrl + D *to deselect a selection.*

MOVE A SELECTION

You can rearrange elements of your image by moving a selection with the Move tool. You can move elements of your image either in the default Background layer or in other layers you create for your image.

If you move elements in the Background layer, Photoshop Elements fills the original location with the current background colour. If you move elements in another layer, Photoshop Elements makes the original location transparent, revealing any underlying layers. See Chapter 5 for more information on layers.

Move a Selection in the Background

1 In the Editor, display the Layers panel.

2 Click the **Background** layer.

A newly imported image has only a Background layer.

3 Use a selection tool to select part of an image.

4 Click the **Move** tool (⊹).

5 Click inside the selection and then drag.

A *Photoshop Elements fills the original location of the selection with the current background colour.*

B *In this example, white is the background colour.*

Move a Selection in a Layer

1 Click a layer in the Layers panel.

2 Use a selection tool to select part of an image.

3 Click the **Move** tool ().

4 Click inside the selection and then drag.

Photoshop Elements moves the selection and fills the original location of the selection with transparent pixels.

Note: *The Background – the default layer in Photoshop Elements – is opaque; other layers can include transparent pixels.*

To move a selection in a straight line, press and hold **Shift** while you drag with the Move tool (■).

You can move several layers at a time. Link the layers you want to move, select one of the linked layers and then move them all with the Move tool (see Chapter 5). You can also hold **Ctrl** and click to select multiple layers in the Layers panel. Using the Move tool moves the selected layers.

COPY AND PASTE A SELECTION

You can copy a selection and make a duplicate of it somewhere else in the image. You may use this technique to retouch an element in your photo by placing good content over bad.

① In the Editor, use a selection tool to select part of an image.

② Click the **Move** tool (⬚).

*Note: You can also click **Copy** and **Paste** in the Edit menu to copy and paste selections.*

③ Press **Alt** while you click and drag the selection.

④ Release the mouse button to drop the selection into place.

Photoshop Elements creates a duplicate of the selection and then places it in the new location.

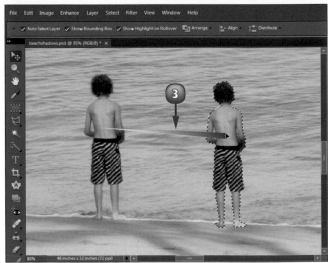

DELETE A SELECTION

You can delete a selection to remove unwanted elements from an image.

1. In the Editor, use a selection tool to select part of an image.

2. Press Delete.

Photoshop Elements deletes the selection.

If you are working in the Background layer, the selection area fills with the background colour; in this example, it is white.

If you are working in a layer other than the Background layer, the selected pixels become transparent and the layers below the selection show through.

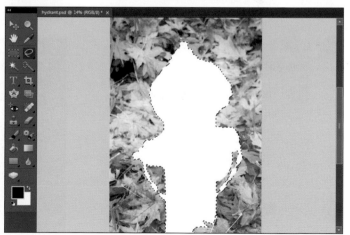

ROTATE A SELECTION

You can rotate a selection to tilt an element or turn it upside down in your image. You may rotate an element to create a better composition or to correct the appearance of an element.

When you rotate a selection in the Background layer, Photoshop Elements replaces the exposed areas that the rotation creates with the current background colour. If you rotate a selection in another layer, the underlying layers appear in the exposed areas. See Chapter 5 for more information on layers.

① In the Editor, use a selection tool to select part of an image.

In this example, content in a layer is selected.

② Click **Image**.

③ Click **Rotate**.

④ Click **Free Rotate Selection**.

You can click other commands under the Rotate menu to rotate your selection in a more constrained way.

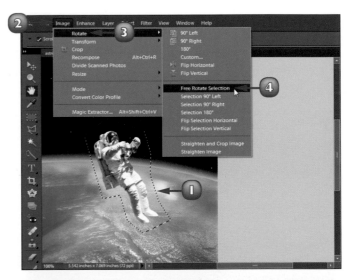

⑤ Click and drag outside the selection.

Ⓐ *You can precisely rotate your selection by typing a value in the degrees field on the Options bar.*

The selection rotates.

⑥ Click ✓ or press Enter to commit to the rotation.

Ⓑ *You can click ◎ or press Esc to cancel the rotation.*

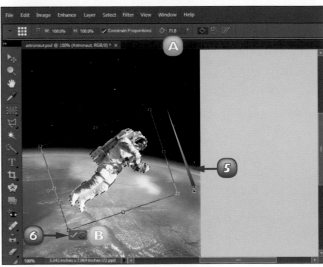

SCALE A SELECTION

You can scale a selection to make it larger or smaller. Scaling enables you to adjust or emphasise parts of your image.

When you scale a selection to a smaller size in the Background layer, Photoshop Elements replaces the exposed areas with the current background colour. If you scale a selection in another layer, exposed areas are transparent and the underlying layers appear. See Chapter 5 for more information on layers.

1 In the Editor, use a selection tool to select part of an image.

In this example, content in a layer is selected.

2 Click **Image**.

3 Click **Resize**.

4 Click **Scale**.

A box with handles on the sides and corners surrounds the selection.

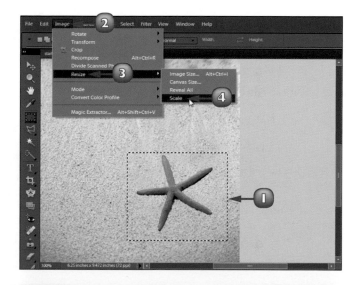

5 Click and drag a handle to scale the selection. Drag a corner handle to scale both the horizontal and vertical axes.

A *You can precisely scale your selection by typing percentage values in the W and H fields.*

B *With Constrain Proportions selected, the height and width change proportionally.*

6 Click ✔ or press Enter to apply the scale effect.

Photoshop Elements scales the selection.

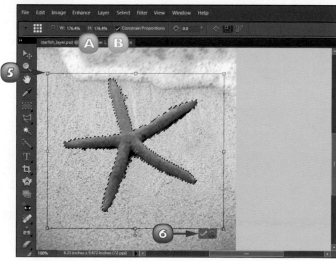

FEATHER THE BORDER OF A SELECTION

You can feather a selection's border to create soft edges. Feathering enables you to control the sharpness of the edges in a selection. You can use this technique with other layers to create a blending effect between the selected area and any underlying layers.

To create a soft edge around an object, you must first select the object, feather the selection border and then delete the part of the image that surrounds your selection.

Feather a Selection

1. In the Editor, use a selection tool to select part of an image.

2. Click **Select**.

3. Click **Feather**.

   You can also press Alt + Ctrl + D to apply the Feather command.

The Feather Selection dialog box opens.

4. Type a pixel value between 0.2 and 250 to determine the softness of the edge.

5. Click **OK**.

Delete the Surrounding Background

 Click **Select**.

 Click **Inverse**.

You can also press Shift + Ctrl + I to apply the Inverse command.

The selection inverts but remains feathered.

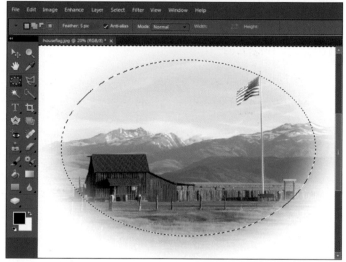

3 Press Delete.

If you are working with the Background layer, the deleted area is filled with the current background colour.

If you are working with a layer other than the Background layer, the deleted area becomes transparent and the layers below show through.

To feather the selection into a coloured background, add a solid-colour fill layer behind your photo and then blend the feathered selection into the new layer. The layer containing the selection appears on top of the solid-colour fill layer and the feathering technique creates a softened blend between the two layers.

STOP *If you apply a command to a feathered selection, Photoshop Elements applies the command only partially to pixels near the edge of the selection. For example, if you remove colour from a selection using the Hue/Saturation command, colour at the feathered edge of the selection is only partially removed.*

CONTENTS

5

LAYER BASICS

You can separate the elements in your image so you can move and transform them independently of one another. You can accomplish this by placing them in different layers.

CREATE AND ADD TO A LAYER

A Photoshop Elements image can consist of multiple layers, with each layer containing different objects in the image.

When you open a digital camera photo or a newly scanned image in Photoshop Elements, it exists as a single layer, known as the *Background* layer. To keep elements in your image independent of one another, you can create separate layers and add objects to them.

You can add content to a new layer by copying and pasting from another image file.

Create a Layer

1. In the Editor, open the Layers panel.

2. Click the layer above which you want to add the new layer.

3. In the Layers panel, click the **Create a New Layer** icon (⬚).

   Alternatively, you can click **Layer**, **New** and then **Layer**.

   A *Photoshop creates a new, transparent layer.*

Note: *To change the name of a layer, see the section "Rename a Layer."*

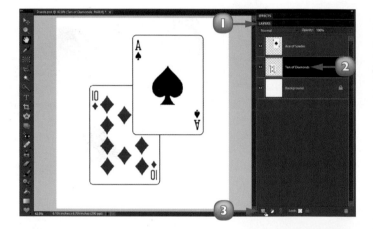

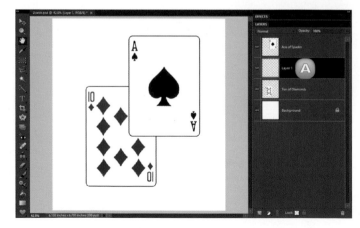

Copy and Paste into a Layer

1 Open another image.

2 Using a selection tool, select the content you want to copy.

3 Click **Edit**.

4 Click **Copy**.

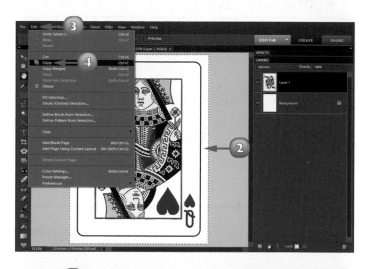

5 Click the tab for the image window where you created the new layer.

6 Click the new layer in the Layers panel.

7 Click **Edit**.

8 Click **Paste**.

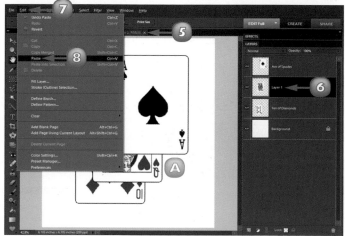

A *The selected content from the other image appears in the new layer.*

Note: *You can also click and drag selections between image windows by using the Move tool () to add content to a new layer.*

 If you have the Background layer selected, you can click Layer, New and then Layer from Background to turn it into a regular layer. The converted layer can be edited just like any other layer.

The Background layer is the default bottom layer. It appears when you create a new image that has a nontransparent background colour or when you import an image from a scanner or digital camera. You can create new layers on top of a Background layer but not below it. Unlike other layers, a Background layer cannot contain transparent pixels.

HIDE A LAYER

You can hide a layer to temporarily remove elements in that layer from view.

Hidden layers do not appear when you print or when you use the Save for Web command.

1. In the Editor, open the Layers panel.

2. Click a layer.

3. Click the **Eye** icon (◉) for the layer.

   The icon disappears.

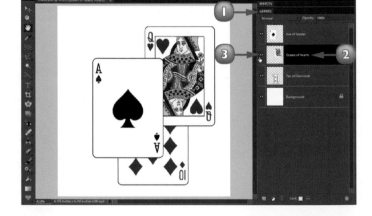

Photoshop hides the layer.

To show one layer and hide all the others, you can press **Alt** and then click the **Eye** icon (◉) for the layer you want to show.

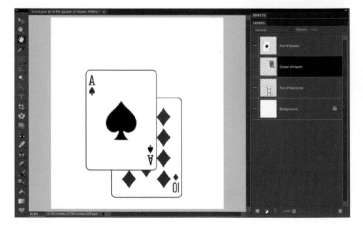

MOVE A LAYER

You can use the Move tool to reposition the elements in one layer without moving elements in other layers.

1 In the Editor, open the Layers panel.

2 Click a layer.

3 Click the **Move** tool (▶).

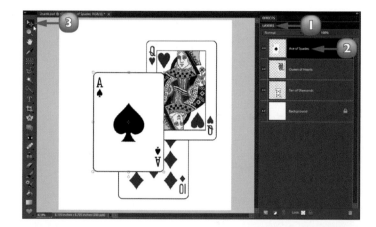

4 Click and drag inside the window.

Content in the selected layer moves.

Content in the other layers does not move.

Note: *To move several layers at the same time, see the section "Link Layers."*

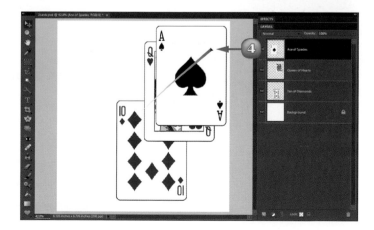

DUPLICATE A LAYER

By duplicating a layer, you can manipulate elements in an image while keeping a copy of their original state.

① In the Editor, open the Layers panel.

② Click a layer.

③ Click and drag the layer to the **Create a New Layer** icon (⬛).

Alternatively, you can click **Layer** and then **Duplicate Layer**; a dialog box opens, asking you to name the layer you want to duplicate.

You can also press `Ctrl`+`J` to duplicate a selected layer in the Layers panel.

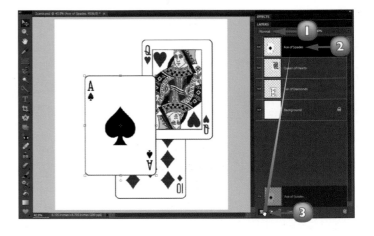

Ⓐ *Photoshop Elements duplicates the selected layer.*

Note: *To rename the duplicate layer, see the section "Rename a Layer."*

Ⓑ *You can test that Photoshop Elements has duplicated the layer by selecting the new layer, clicking the **Move** tool (▣) and then clicking and dragging the layer.*

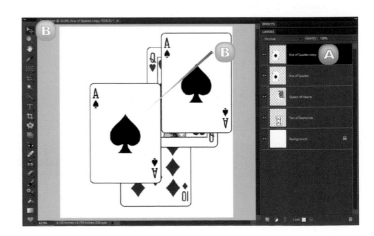

DELETE A LAYER

You can delete a layer when you no longer have a use for its contents.

1 In the Editor, open the Layers panel.

2 Click a layer.

3 Click and drag the layer to the **Trash** icon (🗑).

Alternatively, you can click **Layer** and then **Delete Layer** or you can select a layer and then click the **Trash** icon (🗑). In both cases, a confirmation dialog box opens.

Photoshop Elements deletes the selected layer and the content in the layer disappears from the image window.

Note: *You can hide a layer if you do not want to see it temporarily. See the "Hide a Layer" section.*

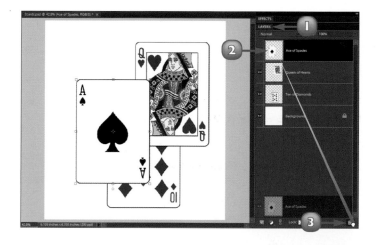

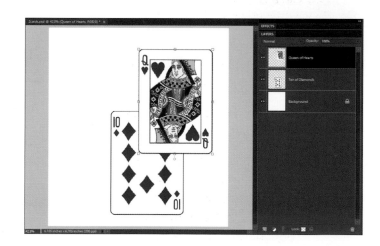

REORDER LAYERS

You can change the order of layers to move elements forward or backward in your image.

Using the Layers Panel

1. In the Editor, open the Layers panel.

2. Click a layer.

3. Click and drag the layer to change its arrangement in the stack.

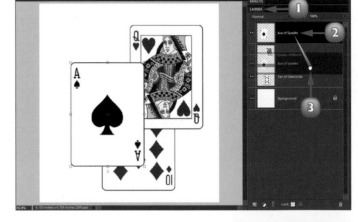

A. The layer assumes its new position in the stack.

B. In this example, the Ace of Spades layer moves down in the stack.

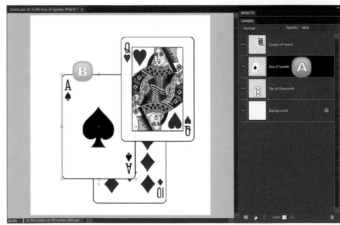

Using the Arrange Commands

① Click a layer.

② Click **Layer**.

③ Click **Arrange**.

④ Click the command for how you want to move the layer.

You can choose **Bring to Front**, **Bring Forward**, **Send Backward**, **Send to Back** or **Reverse**.

Note: *Reverse is only available if more than one layer is selected. You can hold* Ctrl *and click in the Layers panel to select multiple layers.*

In this example, Bring Forward is chosen and the Ace of Spades layer moves to the top of the stack.

Ⓐ *The layer assumes its new position in the stack.*

Note: *You cannot move a layer behind the default Background layer.*

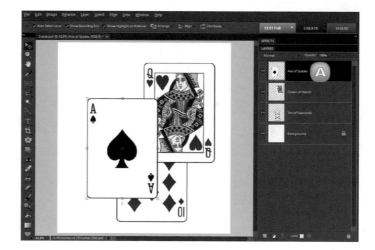

You can shift layers forward and backward in the stack by pressing the following shortcut keys: Ctrl+] *or* Ctrl+[*moves the layer forward or backward one step;* Shift+Ctrl+] *moves the layer to the front and* Shift +Ctrl+[*moves the layer to the back.*

LINK LAYERS

Linking causes different layers to move in unison when you move them with the Move tool.

You may find linking useful when you want to keep elements of an image aligned with one another but do not want to merge their layers. Keeping layers unmerged lets you apply effects to each layer independently.

① In the Editor, open the Layers panel.

② Click one of the layers you want to link.

③ Press Ctrl and then click one or more other layers that you want to link.

④ Click the **Link Layers** tool (▣) in the Layers panel.

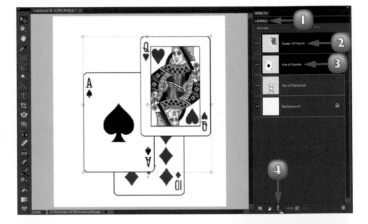

Ⓐ *A linking icon (▣) appears next to each linked layer.*

Ⓑ *To verify that Photoshop Elements has linked the layers, select one of the layers, click the **Move** tool (▶) and then click and drag the layer.*

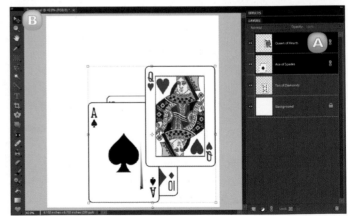

RENAME A LAYER

You can rename a layer to give it a name that describes its content.

1 In the Editor, open the Layers panel.

2 Click a layer.

3 Click **Layer**.

4 Click **Rename Layer**.

The Layer Properties dialog box opens.

5 Type a new name for the layer.

6 Click **OK**.

Ⓐ The name of the layer changes in the Layers panel.

You can also double-click the name of the layer in the Layers panel to edit the name.

CREATE A FILL LAYER

You can create a solid fill layer to place an opaque layer of colour throughout your image. You can use fill layers behind layers containing objects to create all kinds of colour effects in your photos.

1. In the Editor, open the Layers panel.

2. Click the layer you want to appear below the solid colour layer.

3. Click **Layer**.

4. Click **New Fill Layer**.

5. Click **Solid Color**.

   The New Layer dialog box opens.

6. Type a name for the layer or use the default name.

   A. *You can specify a type of blend or opacity setting for the layer.*

7. Click **OK**.

The Color Picker dialog box opens.

 To change the range of colours that appears in the window, click and drag the slider ().

 To select a fill colour, click in the colour window.

10 Click **OK**.

B *Photoshop Elements creates a new layer filled with a solid colour.*

In this example, a solid green layer appears below the card layers.

✓ **To add colour to a specific part of a layer, select the area with a selection tool. Then create the solid fill layer and apply a colour fill as outlined in this section. Photoshop Elements adds colour only inside the selection.**

✓ **In the New Fill Layer menu, you can create gradient fill layers, which apply bands of colour rather than a solid fill. Or you can create a pattern fill layer, which applies a repeating pattern as a fill instead of a solid colour. You can select from a variety of preset gradient effects and patterns.**

CREATE AN ADJUSTMENT LAYER

Adjustment layers let you store colour and tonal changes in a layer instead of having them permanently applied to your image. The information in an adjustment layer is applied to the pixels in the layers below it.

You can use adjustment layers to test an editing technique without applying it to the original layer. Adjustment layers are especially handy for experimenting with colours, tones and brightness settings.

1 In the Editor, open the Layers panel.

2 Click the layer you want to appear below the adjustment layer.

3 Click **Layer**.

4 Click **New Adjustment Layer**.

Note: *You can also click the Create Adjustment Layer icon ( ) in the Layers panel.*

5 Click an adjustment command.

The New Layer dialog box opens.

6 Type a name for the adjustment layer or use the default name.

A *You can specify a type of blend or opacity setting for the layer.*

7 Click **OK**.

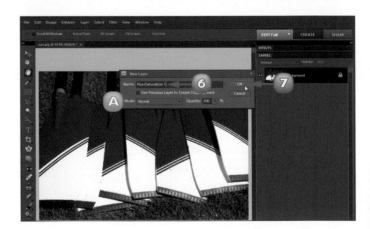

B *Photoshop Elements adds an adjustment layer to the image.*

The panel for the adjustment command appears.

Note: *Depending on the type of adjustment layer you create, different settings appear.*

In this example, an adjustment layer is created that changes the hue and saturation.

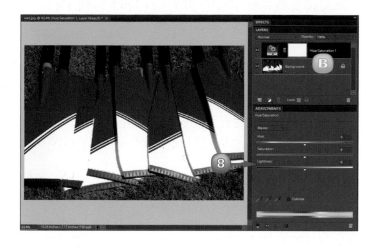

8 Click and drag the sliders () or type values to adjust the settings.

You can see the adjustments take effect in the workspace.

C *Photoshop Elements applies the effect to the layers that are below the adjustment layer.*

You can double-click the adjustment layer to make changes to the settings.

To apply an adjustment layer to only part of an image, select an area with a selection tool. Create the adjustment layer. Photoshop Elements applies the adjustments only to the selection in the underlying layers.

CONTENTS

6

RETOUCHING PHOTOS

Do you need to fix a photo fast? This chapter offers you all kinds of techniques for retouching your digital photos, including correcting common colour problems, making flaws disappear and rearranging objects.

USE THE GUIDED EDIT FACILITY

You can remove blemishes and unwanted objects using the step-by-step instructions and adjustments in the Guided Edit view of Photoshop Elements.

You can retouch photos in Guided Edit using the Spot Healing Brush or the Healing Brush. Both remove imperfections by copying from unblemished areas of your photo.

Guided Edit offers you a Zoom tool and Hand tool for adjusting your image and locating objects.

1 In the Editor, click the EDIT tab and then click **EDIT Guided**.

The Guided Edit view opens.

A Make sure the Guided Activities list is open. You can click the arrow to open it (▶ changes to ▼).

2 Click **Touch Up Scratches, Blemishes or Tear Marks**.

Retouch a Small Area

3 Click the **Spot Healing Brush** ( ).

4 Click and drag the slider ( ) to choose a brush size between 1 and 500.

Note: Select a brush size that covers the area you plan to touch up.

B You can also type a value for the brush size.

5 Click an object in your image.

Photoshop Elements blends the object with nearby pixels.

Retouch a Larger Area

3 Click the **Healing Brush** ().

4 Click and drag the slider (⬛) to choose a brush size between 1 and 2500.

Note: *Select a brush size that is slightly smaller than the area you plan to touch up.*

C *You can also type a value for the brush size.*

5 Press **Alt** and then click an unblemished area of your image that has a similar colour and texture.

6 Click and drag across an object in your image.

Photoshop Elements covers the object with pixels from the unblemished area.

7 Click Done to return to the main Guided Edit view.

Viewing the Objects to Retouch

1 Click the **Zoom** tool (🔍).

2 Click inside your image to zoom in.

3 Click the **Hand** tool (✋).

4 Click and drag to move your image horizontally and vertically.

QUICK FIX A PHOTO

You can use the Quick Fix view in Photoshop Elements to make fast corrections to your photos in one convenient window. You can use tools to correct common colour problems in your photos, such as making sky bluer and whitening teeth.

The Quick Fix pane consists of a variety of panels: the Smart Fix panel automatically corrects lighting, colour and contrast; the Lighting panel adjusts the contrast and exposure; the Color panel fixes colour problems; the Balance panel fixes the colour balance and the Detail panel sharpens the image.

Select a Quick Fix View

1 In the Editor, click the EDIT tab ⏷ and then click **EDIT Quick**.

The Quick Fix pane opens.

2 Click to choose a view mode:

After Only shows your changes.

Before Only shows the unedited photo.

The *Before and After* views show both the original image and the edited image side by side or stacked.

Use the Smart Fix Panel

1 Click and drag the **Amount** slider (▮).

A *Photoshop Elements shows the adjustments immediately.*

B *You can click **Auto** to have Photoshop Elements automatically adjust your image.*

C *You can click **Reset** to return to the original settings.*

2 Click ✓ or press Enter to accept.

Add Blue to Skies

① In the Editor, open a photo that includes a dull-coloured sky.

② Click the EDIT tab ▾ and then click **EDIT Quick**.

③ Click the **Make Dull Skies Blue** tool (🔲).

Ⓐ *You can click here to adjust the brush size.*

④ Click and drag over the sky.

Photoshop Elements selects the sky and boosts the blue colour.

Ⓑ *You can click* **Reset** *to revert the photo to its previous state.*

Whiten Teeth

① Open a photo that includes teeth.

② Click the **Whiten Teeth** tool (🔲).

Ⓐ *You can click here to adjust the brush size.*

③ Click and drag over teeth in the photo.

Photoshop Elements whitens the teeth, decreasing any colourcast they might have.

 If you do not like the result of a Quick Fix, you can click **Edit** *and then click* **Undo.**

 The tools in the other panels are used in the same way.

REMOVE RED EYE

You can use the Red Eye Removal tool to remove the red eye colour that a camera flash can cause.

Red eye is a common problem in snapshots taken indoors with a flash. Light from the flash reflects off the back of the subject's eyes, creating the red appearance. Using the Red Eye Removal tool, you can edit the eye to change its colour without changing image details.

① In the Editor, click the **Red Eye Removal** tool (▨).

② Click here and then drag the slider (▮) to control the size of the area to correct.

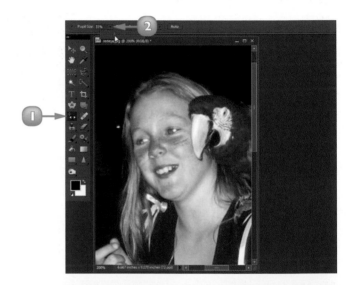

③ Click here and then drag the slider (▮) to the darkness setting you want.

④ Click the eye you want to fix.

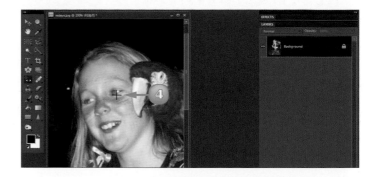

⑤ Release the mouse button.

Photoshop Elements repairs the eye colour.

Note: *If you need to change the settings, you can click* **Undo** *() to undo the colour change.*

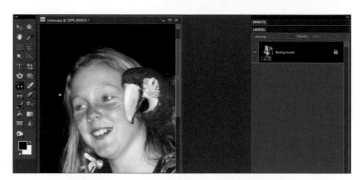

Remove Green Eye from Pets

① Click the **Burn** tool (■).

② Set your brush style and size options.

③ Select **Highlights** in the Range menu.

④ Click the eye you want to darken.

Photoshop Elements darkens the eye. You can click as many times as needed to get the desired colour.

RETOUCH WITH THE CLONE STAMP TOOL

You can clean up small flaws or erase elements in your image with the Clone Stamp tool. The tool copies information from one area of an image to another. For example, you can use the Clone Stamp tool to remove unwanted blemishes of all kinds by cloning an area near the flaw and then stamping over the flaw.

① In the Editor, click the **Clone Stamp** tool (■).

② Click here to choose a brush size and type.

Ⓐ *You can also set an exact brush size here.*

You can change the brush size while using the tool by pressing [and].

③ Click here to choose an opacity, which determines whether the tool covers an area completely or partially.

You can also type a value for the opacity.

④ Press and hold Alt and then click the area of the image from which you want to copy.

In this example, the Clone Stamp is used to remove a handhold from a climbing wall.

5 Click and drag on the area of the photo that you want to correct.

Photoshop Elements copies the cloned area to where you click and drag.

6 Continue clicking new areas to clone and drag over the area as many times as needed to achieve the desired effect.

You can click **Undo** (⟲) to undo the tool's effects.

 To erase elements from your image with the Clone Stamp without leaving a trace, try the following: clone between areas of similar colour and texture; apply the stamp more subtly by lowering its opacity; use a soft-edged brush shape.

 You can use the Pattern Stamp to paint repeating patterns on your images. Right-click on the Clone Stamp tool (▣) and then click Pattern Stamp (▣). Select a pattern, brush style and brush size and then stamp the pattern on your photo.

CORRECT A SPOT

You can use the Spot Healing Brush to quickly repair flaws in a photo. The tool works well on small spots or blemishes on both solid and textured backgrounds.

The tool's Proximity Match setting analyses pixels surrounding the selected area and replaces the area with a patch of similar pixels. The Create Texture setting replaces the area with a blend of surrounding pixels.

① In the Editor, click the **Spot Healing Brush** tool (🖌️).

② Click here to choose a brush size and type.

Ⓐ *You can also set an exact brush size here.*

③ Click here to choose the type of healing effect you want to apply (● changes to ○).

Proximity Match applies pixels from around the selected area.

Create Texture applies a blend of pixels from the selected area.

④ Click and drag over the spot you want to correct.

You may have to click and drag several times to get the effect you want.

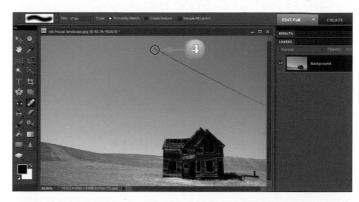

Photoshop Elements replaces the selected area with pixels similar to those nearby.

You can click **Undo** () to undo the change.

Correct Larger Areas of a Photo

① Right-click on the **Spot Healing Brush** tool (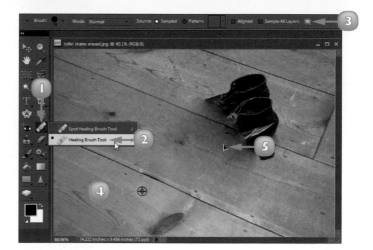).

② Click the **Healing Brush** tool (🖌️).

③ Adjust the tool's settings.

④ Press and hold **Alt** and then click the area you want to clone.

⑤ Drag over the problem area to blend the cloned pixels into the new area.

SHARPEN AN IMAGE

You can use the Adjust Sharpness dialog box to sharpen an image suffering from focus problems. The tool lets you control the amount of sharpening you apply.

To apply the filter to just part of your image, you can select that part with a selection tool.

① In the Editor, select the layer to which you want to apply the enhancement.

In this example, the image only has the Background layer.

② Click **Enhance**.

③ Click **Adjust Sharpness**.

The Adjust Sharpness dialog box opens.

Ⓐ A preview area displays the filter's effect.

Ⓑ You can click the **Preview** check box to preview the effect in the main window (■ changes to ✓).

④ Click minus (⊟) or plus (⊞) to zoom out or in.

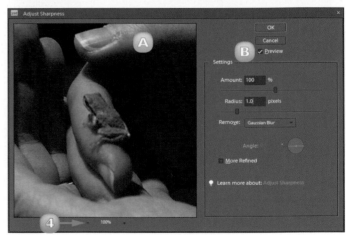

5 Click and drag the sliders (⬛) or type values to control the sharpening you apply to the image.

C *Amount controls the overall amount of sharpening.*

D *You can confine sharpening to edges in the image using a low Radius setting or add sharpening across the entire image using a high Radius setting.*

E *You can click here to remove a specific type of blur in the image. The default is Gaussian Blur.*

6 Click **OK**.

Photoshop Elements applies the enhancement.

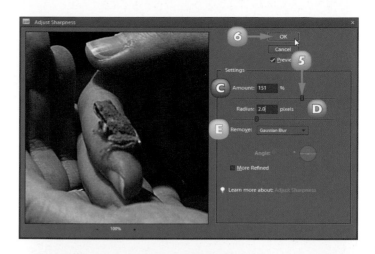

 Sharpening an image after you change its size can be a good idea. Changing an image's size, especially enlarging, can add blurring. Adjusting sharpness can also help clarify scanned images. Although the tool cannot perform a miracle and make an unfocused image completely clear, it can sharpen slightly blurred images or blurring caused by applying other filters.

 The Auto button on the Sharpen panel in the Quick Fix window sharpens an image by a preset amount. If you use the Quick Fix window to retouch a photo, you can easily apply the Auto Sharpen command. However, you can fine-tune the sharpening effects when using the Adjust Sharpness dialog box.

CONTENTS

7

ENHANCING CONTRAST AND EXPOSURE

Does your photo suffer from shadows that are too dark or highlights that are too light? Or perhaps you have an old photo in which the entire image is faded? You can correct tone, contrast, exposure and lighting problems by using several nifty tools in Photoshop Elements. This chapter shows you how.

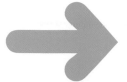

ENHANCE LIGHTING WITH GUIDED EDIT

You can fix simple lighting problems in your images by using the step-by-step instructions and adjustments in the Guided Edit interface in Photoshop Elements. This feature lets you compare before-and-after versions of an image as you change the lighting.

The Smart Fix feature of Photoshop Elements automatically optimises the light and colour at the same time; it can be a good first step in trying to fix exposure problems.

① In the Editor, click **EDIT Guided**.

The Guided Edit view opens.

Ⓐ *Make sure the Lighting and Exposure list is open. You can click here to open it (▶ changes to ▼).*

② Click **Lighten or Darken**.

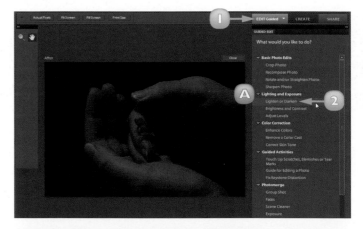

Ⓑ *You can click **Auto** to have Photoshop Elements automatically adjust the lighting using its built-in optimisation routines.*

③ Click the **View** button (▣) to open Before and After views of the image (▣ changes to ▣).

4. Click and drag the slider () to lighten shadows in the image.

5. Click and drag this slider to darken highlights in the image.

6. Click and drag this slider to increase or decrease the contrast in the image.

   You can also type values for the shadows, highlights and contrast.

7. Click **Done**.

   Photoshop Elements enhances the lighting in the image.

Note: *Click the EDIT tab* ▾ *and then EDIT Full to switch to the Full Edit view.*

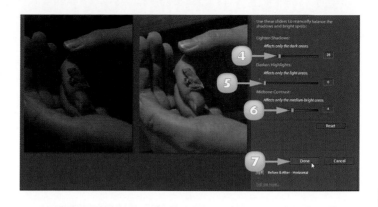

Adjust Lighting and Colour in One Step

1. Click **Enhance**.

2. Click **Adjust Smart Fix**.

   The Adjust Smart Fix dialog box opens.

3. Click and drag the slider (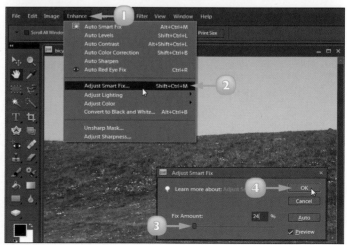) to control the strength of the adjustment.

4. Click **OK**.

   Photoshop Elements applies the adjustment.

ADJUST LIGHTING LEVELS

You can use the Levels dialog box to fine-tune shadows, highlights and midtones in your image. Input sliders enable you to manipulate the tonal qualities and colour balance of an image and output sliders let you adjust contrast.

You can adjust levels in part of your image by making a selection or selecting a layer before executing the command. For more on making selections, see Chapter 4. For more on working with layers, see Chapter 5.

1 In the Editor, click **Enhance**.

2 Click **Adjust Lighting**.

3 Click **Levels**.

The Levels dialog box opens.

4 Make sure to click the **Preview** check box (■ changes to ☑).

The Preview option enables you to see your adjustments as you make them.

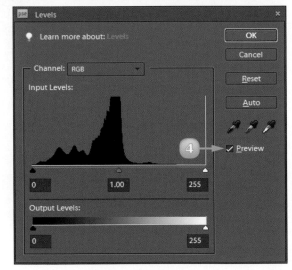

120

⑤ Click and drag this slider (■) to darken shadows and increase contrast.

⑥ Click and drag this slider (▲) to adjust the midtones of the image.

⑦ Click and drag this slider (▲) to lighten the bright areas of the image and increase contrast.

You can also type values for the contrast and midtones.

Photoshop Elements displays a preview of the adjustments in the workspace.

⑧ Click and drag this slider (■) to the right to lighten the image.

⑨ Click and drag this slider (▲) to the left to darken the image.

⑩ Click **OK**.

Photoshop Elements applies the adjustments.

 *You can automatically adjust the brightness levels of an image. Click **Enhance** and then **Auto Levels**. Photoshop Elements sets the lightest pixels to white, the darkest pixels to black and then redistributes the intermediate values proportionately throughout the rest of the image.*

 The Levels dialog box includes three Eyedropper tools, one each for the darkest (🖋), midtone (🖋) and lightest tones (🖋). You can click the Eyedropper tool for the tone you want to set and then click the appropriate pixels in your image.

ADJUST SHADOWS AND HIGHLIGHTS

You can use the Shadows and Highlights feature to make quick adjustments to the dark and light areas of your image. This feature is less complicated than the Levels tool but is also less flexible.

You can adjust shadows and highlights in part of your image by making a selection (see Chapter 4) or selecting a layer (see Chapter 5) before executing the command.

① In the Editor, click **Enhance**.

② Click **Adjust Lighting**.

③ Click **Shadows/Highlights**.

The Shadows/Highlights dialog box opens.

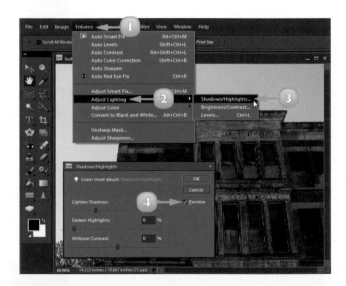

④ Make sure to click the **Preview** check box (■ changes to ✓).

The Preview option lets you view and verify your adjustments as you make them.

⑤ Click and drag the slider (■) to lighten shadows in the image.

⑥ Click and drag this slider to darken highlights in the image.

⑦ Click and drag this slider to adjust midtone contrast in the image.

You can also type values for the shadows, highlights and contrast.

⑧ Click **OK**.

Photoshop Elements applies the adjustments.

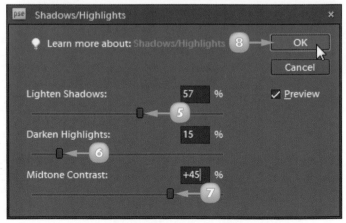

 If you press and hold Alt, Cancel changes to Reset. Click Reset to return the settings to their default values.

ADJUST BRIGHTNESS AND CONTRAST

You can use the Brightness/Contrast dialog box to adjust the brightness and contrast levels in a photo or a selected portion of a photo. *Brightness* refers to the intensity of the lighter pixels in an image and *contrast* refers to the relative difference between dark and light areas in an image.

To make more complex adjustments to the tonal qualities in an image, use the Levels dialog box. You can also use the Adjust Color Curves command, which is covered in Chapter 8.

① In the Editor, click **Enhance**.

② Click **Adjust Lighting**.

③ Click **Brightness/Contrast**.

The Brightness/Contrast dialog box opens.

Ⓐ The Preview check box is selected by default.

④ Click and drag the **Brightness** slider (🖼) right to lighten the image or left to darken the image.

Ⓑ You can also type a number from 150 to -150 to lighten or darken the image.

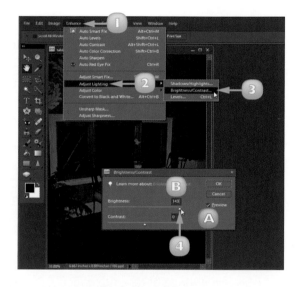

⑤ Click and drag the **Contrast** slider (◼) right to increase or left to decrease contrast.

Ⓒ You can also type a number from 1 to 100 to increase contrast or from -1 to -50 to decrease contrast.

⑥ Click **OK**.

Photoshop Elements applies the adjustments to the image, selection or layer.

LIGHTEN AREAS WITH THE DODGE TOOL

You can use the Dodge tool to quickly brighten a specific area of an image. *Dodge* is a photographic term that describes the diffusing of light when developing a film negative. For example, you can tweak a dark area of an image by brushing over the area with the Dodge tool.

You can fine-tune the effects of the Dodge tool by specifying what to correct – midtones, shadows or highlights – and specifying the strength of the lightening effect. You can use the tool in only part of your image by making a selection (see Chapter 4) before executing the command.

1 In the Editor, right-click on the **Sponge** tool ().

2 Click the **Dodge** tool (■).

3 Click here to choose the brush you want to use.

> **A** You can also select an exact brush size here.

Note: You can change the brush size while using the tool by pressing [and].

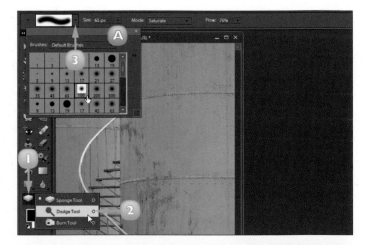

> **B** You can click here to choose the range of tones to affect.

> **C** You can click here to choose the tool's exposure or strength.

4 Click and drag the mouse pointer (○) over the area you want to lighten.

Photoshop Elements lightens the area.

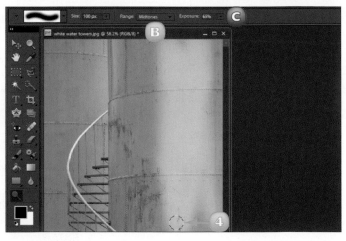

 You can drag repeatedly over the area you want to correct to gradually brighten the area.

 You can apply the Dodge tool with the Range set to Highlights to brighten the lighter areas of an object in your image.

DARKEN AREAS WITH THE BURN TOOL

You can use the Burn tool to darken a specific area of an image. *Burn* is a photographic term that describes the focusing of light when developing a film negative. For example, you can tweak a bright area of an image by brushing over the area with the Burn tool.

You can fine-tune the effects of the Burn tool by specifying what to correct – midtones, shadows or highlights – and specifying the strength of the darkening effect. You can use the tool in only part of your image by making a selection (see Chapter 4) before executing the command.

1 In the Editor, right-click on the **Sponge** tool (⬤).

2 Click the **Burn** tool (⬤).

3 Click here to choose the brush you want to use.

   You can also select the range of colours you want to affect and the tool's exposure or strength.

4 Click and drag the mouse pointer (○) over the area you want to darken.

   Photoshop Elements darkens the area. In this example, a shadow is cast against the ground and wall.

Note: *If you continue to click areas or click and drag over an area, the area is darkened more with each application of the tool.*

 You can use the Burn tool with the Range set to Shadows to add shadows to the shaded side of an object.

CONTENTS

8

ENHANCING COLOURS

Do your photos suffer from faded colours or unattractive colourcasts? This chapter shows you how to use the tools in Photoshop Elements to correct colour problems in your images by adding, removing or shifting colours.

ENHANCE COLOURS WITH GUIDED EDIT

You can enhance or shift the colours in your images by using the step-by-step instructions and adjustments in the Photoshop Elements Guided Edit interface. The interface lets you compare before and after versions of an image as you adjust the colours.

① In the Editor, click the EDIT tab 🔽 and then click **EDIT Guided**.

The Guided Edit interface opens.

Ⓐ *Make sure the Color Correction list is open. You can click the arrow to open it (▶ changes to ▼).*

② Click **Enhance Colors**.

Ⓑ *You can click **Auto** to have Photoshop Elements automatically balance the colours and contrast by using its built-in optimisation routines.*

③ Click the **View** button (▦) to open Before and After views of the image (▦ changes to ▦).

④ Click and drag the **Hue** slider (⬛) to shift the colours in the image.

⑤ Click and drag the **Saturation** slider to change the colour intensity in the image.

⑥ Click and drag the **Lightness** slider to change the lightness of the colours in the image.

You can also type values for the hue, saturation and lightness.

⑦ Click **Done**.

Photoshop Elements adjusts the colours in the image.

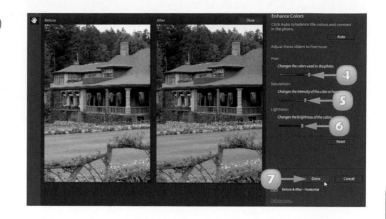

129

 You can limit the adjustments to a specific type of colour. Click **Enhance,** *click* **Adjust Color** *and then click* **Adjust Hue/Saturation.** *Click the dropdown arrow to choose a colour type. Click and drag the sliders (⊡) to make adjustments. Click* **OK.**

CHAPTER 8 ENHANCING COLOURS

ADJUST SKIN COLOUR

You can improve skin colours that may appear tinted or washed out in your images. After you sample an area of skin with the eyedropper, Photoshop Elements adjusts the skin colour to make it look more natural. Photoshop Elements also adjusts other colours in the image based on the sampled skin.

1 In the Editor, click **Enhance**.

2 Click **Adjust Color**.

3 Click **Adjust Color for Skin Tone**.

The Adjust Color for Skin Tone dialog box opens.

A *The mouse pointer (⬚) changes to an eyedropper (✎).*

4 Click an area of skin in your image.

Photoshop Elements adjusts the skin tones and other colours in your image.

5 Click and drag the **Tan** slider (■) to adjust the level of brown in the skin tones.

6 Click and drag the **Blush** slider (■) to adjust the level of red in the skin tones.

7 Click and drag the **Temperature** slider (■) to adjust the overall colouring of the skin tones.

8 Click **OK**.

Photoshop Elements makes adjustments to the skin in the image.

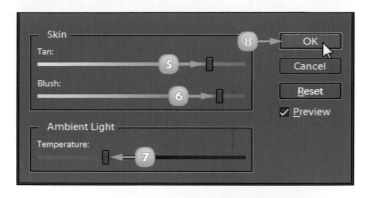

 Photoshop Elements can adjust a photo based on the mix of highlights, midtones and shadows in the image. It maps the darkest and lightest pixels based on a default set of values and neutralises the midtones. Click the layer you want to adjust. Click Enhance. Click Auto Color Correction.

ADJUST COLOUR WITH THE SPONGE TOOL

You can use the Sponge tool to make simple adjustments to the colour saturation or colour intensity of a specific area of an image. For example, you may want to make a person's clothing appear more colourful or tone down an element that is too colourful.

Decrease Saturation

1 In the Editor, click the **Sponge** tool (⬤).

Note: *You may need to click and hold the Dodge or Burn tool and then select the Sponge tool from the menu.*

2 Click here to choose the brush style you want to use.

A *You can also click here and then drag the slider (■) to set a brush size.*

3 Click here and then choose **Desaturate**.

4 Click and drag the mouse pointer (○) to decrease the saturation of an area of the image.

In this example, a section of the hydrant is desaturated. To confine the effect to a particular area, you can make a selection prior to applying the tool.

Increase Saturation

① In the Editor, click the **Sponge** tool (◼).

② Choose the brush style you want to use.

③ Click the Mode dropdown and then choose **Saturate**.

④ Click and drag the mouse pointer (○) to increase the saturation of an area of the image.

In this example, the colours of a barn door and a trash can are intensified.

To confine the effect to a particular area, you can make a selection prior to applying the tool.

Ⓐ *You can adjust the strength of the Sponge tool by clicking here and moving the slider (◼) between 1% and 100%.*

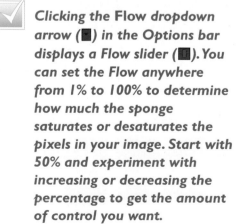

✓ **Clicking the Flow dropdown arrow (◼) in the Options bar displays a Flow slider (◼). You can set the Flow anywhere from 1% to 100% to determine how much the sponge saturates or desaturates the pixels in your image. Start with 50% and experiment with increasing or decreasing the percentage to get the amount of control you want.**

✓ **The Brushes panel displays a variety of brush styles with soft, hard and shaped edges. To blend your sponging effect into the surrounding pixels, select a soft-edge brush style. To make your sponging effect appear more distinct, use a hard-edge brush style. Shaped edges can help you produce textured effects.**

CORRECT COLOUR PROBLEMS

You can use the Color Variations feature to quickly fix colourcasts and other colour problems in a photo. Colourcasts result from unfavourable lighting conditions. For example, when you shoot a subject under fluorescent lights, your photograph may take on a greenish colour. Age can also add casts to a photo.

If you make a selection (see Chapter 4) before performing the Color Variations command, you affect only the selected pixels. Similarly, if you have a multilayered image (see Chapter 5), your adjustments affect only the selected layer.

1 In the Editor, click **Enhance**.

2 Click **Adjust Color**.

3 Click **Color Variations**.

To apply colour corrections to a particular layer, select the layer before opening the Color Variations dialog box.

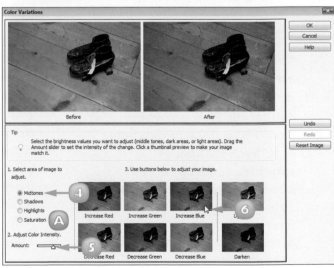

The Color Variations dialog box opens.

4 Choose a tonal range to apply effects to the different tones of your image.

A *Alternatively, you can click the **Saturation** radio button (◎ changes to ◉).*

5 Click and drag the slider (🖫) left to make small adjustments or right to make large adjustments.

6 To add or subtract a colour, click one of the thumbnails.

B *The result of the adjustment appears in the After preview.*

To increase the effect, click the thumbnail again.

C *You can increase the brightness by clicking* **Lighten**.

D *You can decrease the brightness of the image by clicking* **Darken**.

7 Continue adjusting other tonal ranges as needed.

8 Click **OK**.

Photoshop Elements makes the colour adjustments to the image.

In this example, the objects in the photo are overly yellow. The Color Variations dialog box enables you to adjust the colour and bring out the shadowing.

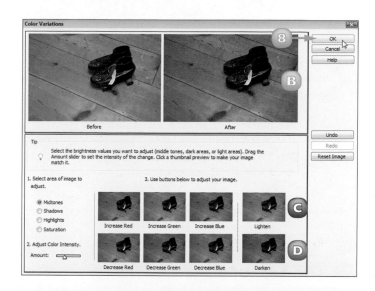

 *Click **Undo** to cancel the last adjustment.*

 *Click **Reset Image** to return the image to its original state, as it looked before you opened the dialog box.*

 *If you have clicked a Decrease thumbnail image, you can click the corresponding **Increase** thumbnail image to undo the effect. If you have clicked an Increase thumbnail image, you can click the corresponding Decrease thumbnail image to undo the effect.*

REPLACE A COLOUR

The Replace Color command lets you change one or more colours in your image by using the hue, saturation and lightness controls.

If you make a selection (see Chapter 4) before executing the Replace Color command, only the selected pixels are affected. Similarly, if you have a multilayered image, your adjustments affect only the selected layer (see Chapter 5).

① In the Editor, click **Enhance**.

② Click **Adjust Color**.

③ Click **Replace Color**.

To apply colour corrections to a particular layer, select the layer before opening the Replace Color dialog box.

The Replace Color dialog box opens. The mouse pointer (⬚) changes to an eyedropper (✐).

④ Click in the image to select a colour to replace.

Ⓐ *Photoshop Elements turns the selected colour to white in the preview window.*

⑤ Click and drag the **Fuzziness** slider (■) to control the degree of tolerance for related colours within the image or selection.

Dragging to the right selects more colour and dragging to the left selects less colour.

You can also type a value for the fuzziness.

6 Click and drag the sliders (■) to change the colours inside the selected area.

You can also type values for the hue, saturation and lightness.

Note: *For more on these controls, see the section "Enhance Colours with Guided Edit."*

7 Click **OK**.

Photoshop Elements replaces the selected colour.

You can press Shift *and then click inside your image to add other colours to your selection. If you are viewing the Selection preview, the white area inside the preview box increases as you click. To deselect colours from your selection, press* Alt *and then click a colour inside your image.*

TURN A COLOUR PHOTO INTO BLACK AND WHITE

You can turn a colour photo into a black-and-white photo to create a dramatic effect or before publishing the photo in a newsletter or brochure that does not use colour.

Photoshop Elements enables you to adjust the contribution of different colours to the effect. Working with channels allows you to choose which colours become black and white. You can leave your image in RGB colour mode and desaturate the colour channels by using the Hue/Saturation dialog box.

You may want to copy the colour image file before making the change and saving so the full-colour original file remains intact.

1. In the Editor, click **Enhance**.

2. Click **Convert to Black and White**.

   To confine the conversion to a particular area, you can make a selection prior to applying the command.

The Convert to Black and White dialog box opens.

3. Click a style.

   Ⓐ Photoshop Elements displays a preview of the black-and-white version.

4 You can click and drag the sliders (▉) to adjust the contributions of the original colours to the final black-and-white version.

5 You can also click this slider to increase or decrease the contrast.

6 Click **OK**.

Photoshop Elements converts the image to black and white.

Remove Colour from a Single Colour Channel

1 Click **Enhance**, **Adjust Color** and then **Adjust Hue/ Saturation**.

2 In the Hue/Saturation dialog box, click here and choose a colour channel.

3 Drag the **Saturation** slider (圄) to the left.

You can also type a value for the saturation.

4 Click **OK** to desaturate the colour channel.

ADD COLOUR TO A BLACK-AND-WHITE PHOTO

You can enhance a black-and-white photo by adding colour with the painting tools in Photoshop Elements. For example, you can add colour to a baby's cheeks or to articles of clothing. To add colour, you must first make sure your image's mode is RGB Color.

You can retain the original black-and-white version of your photo by making colour changes on duplicate or adjustment layers (see Chapter 5).

You can change layer opacity in the Layers panel to make the colour more transparent.

① In the Editor, click **Image**.

② Click **Mode**.

③ Click **RGB Color**.

If your image has multiple layers, you may need to flatten the layers before proceeding. In the prompt box that opens, click **Flatten**.

④ Duplicate the Background layer.

⑤ Click the **Brush** tool (🖌).

⑥ Click the foreground colour.

⑦ In the Color Picker dialog box, click a colour range.

⑧ Click a colour.

You can also type values for a colour.

⑨ Click **OK**.

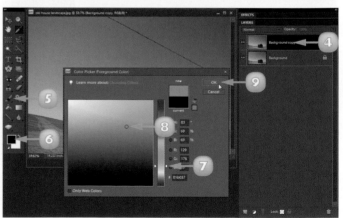

10 Click here to set the blending mode to Colour. This enables you to retain the lighting details of the objects that you paint over.

To confine the effect to a particular area, you can make a selection prior to applying the tool.

11 Click and drag to paint the colour on the photo.

Photoshop Elements applies the colour to the black-and-white image.

This example shows colour added to a grassy area.

A *You can click the visibility icon (■) to hide the layer with the colour and revert the image to black and white.*

Tone Down a Layer Colour

1 Click the layer containing the colour you want to edit.

2 Click here and then click and drag the slider (■) that appears.

Photoshop Elements automatically adjusts the colour as you drag.

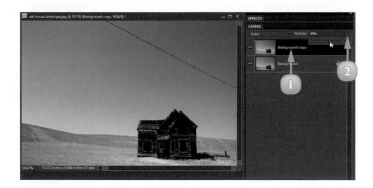

ADJUST COLOUR BY USING COLOUR CURVES

You can manipulate the tones and contrast of your image with the Color Curves dialog box. In the dialog box, the colours in the image are represented by a sloping line graph. The top-right part of the line represents the highlights, the middle part the midtones and the bottom-left part the shadows.

You can adjust curves in just a part of your image by making a selection or selecting a layer before executing the command.

1 In the Editor, click **Enhance**.

2 Click **Adjust Color**.

3 Click **Adjust Color Curves**.

The Adjust Color Curves dialog box opens.

4 Click a style.

A Photoshop Elements displays a preview of the adjusted version.

B The curves graph changes depending on the style.

In this example, choosing the Increase Contrast style gives the graph a slight S shape.

⑤ You can click and drag the sliders (■) to make more adjustments to the tones and contrast in the image.

⑥ Click **OK**.

Photoshop Elements applies the adjustment to the image.

Give Colours an Out-of-this-world Appearance

① In the Editor, click **Enhance, Adjust Color** and **Adjust Color Curves**.

② Click **Solarize** in the Select a Style menu.

③ Click **OK** to apply the effect.

Note: *Photoshop Elements has a Solarize filter that generates a similar effect.*

CONTENTS

9

PAINTING AND DRAWING ON PHOTOS

Want to add extra elements to your photos, such as lines, shapes or solid areas of colour? Photoshop Elements offers a variety of tools you can use to paint and draw on your images as well as add shapes and colours. This chapter introduces you to some of those tools and their many uses.

SET THE FOREGROUND AND BACKGROUND COLOURS

You can select colours to use with many of the painting and drawing tools in Photoshop Elements by setting the foreground and background colours. The Brush and Pencil tools apply the foreground colour and the Eraser tool applies the background colour.

See the section "Add Colour with the Brush Tool" for more on how to paint on a photo. See the section "Erase an Area" for more on using the Eraser.

Set the Foreground Colour

1 In the Editor, click the **Foreground Color** box (■).

The Color Picker dialog box opens.

2 Click and drag the colour slider (▶▭◀) to select a colour range.

3 Click a colour.

You can click outside the dialog box, in the image window, to select a colour from your photo.

You can also type values for a colour.

4 Click **OK**.

A The selected colour appears in the Foreground Color box.

B When you use a tool that applies the foreground colour, Photoshop Elements paints or draws the foreground colour on the photo.

This example uses the Brush tool.

Note: For more on painting tools, see the section "Add Colour with the Brush Tool."

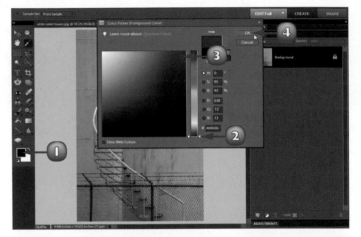

Set the Background Colour

1 Click the **Background Color** box (□).

The Color Picker dialog box opens.

2 Click and drag the colour slider (◀■■▶) to select a colour range.

3 Click a colour.

You can click outside the dialog box, in the image window, to select a colour from your photo.

You can also type values for a colour.

4 Click **OK**.

A *The selected colour appears in the Background Color box.*

B *When you use a tool that applies the background colour, such as the Eraser tool, Photoshop Elements applies the background colour on the photo.*

The Eraser tool applies colour only in the Background layer; in other layers, the Eraser tool turns pixels transparent.

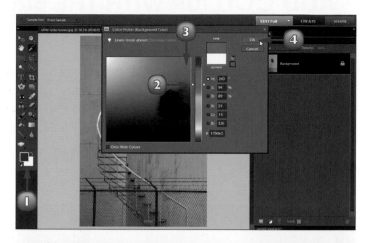

  To reset the foreground and background colours to black and white, click the Default button (■) or press D. You can also click the Switch icon (■) or press X to swap the foreground and background colours.

  *You can select a colour to paint or draw on your photo from the Color Swatches panel, which includes a set of commonly used colours. To view the panel, click **Window** and then **Color Swatches**. Click the colour you want to use as the Foreground Color. To set the Background Color, press **Ctrl** and click a colour in the panel.*

147

CHAPTER 9 PAINTING AND DRAWING ON PHOTOS

ADD COLOUR WITH THE BRUSH TOOL

You can use the Brush tool to add patches of solid colour to your image. You can use the tool to cover unwanted elements or change the appearance of clothing or a backdrop. When applying the Brush tool, you can control the size of the brushstrokes by choosing a brush size. For realistic results, turn on the Airbrush feature to apply a softer line of colour.

To limit where the brush applies colour, create a selection before using the tool.

① In the Editor, click the **Brush** tool (▰).

② Click the **Foreground Color** box (■) to select a colour with which to paint.

You can also press and hold Alt and then click inside your image to select a colour.

③ Click **OK**.

④ Click here and then choose a brush size and type.

Ⓐ *To set a brush size, you can also click here and adjust the slider that appears.*

Note: *You can also type a brush size.*

⑤ Press Enter to close the Brushes menu.

6 Click and drag the mouse pointer
(○) on the image.

Photoshop Elements applies
colour to the image.

7 Click here to reduce the opacity
of the paint effect.

You can also type a value for the
opacity.

8 Click and drag the mouse pointer
(○) on the image.

Photoshop Elements applies
transparent colour to the image.

To undo the most recent
brushstroke, you can click **Edit**
and then **Undo Brush Tool** or
click the **Undo** button (◨).

 *To paint thin lines, use the
Pencil tool (▨). Like the Brush
tool, the Pencil applies the
foreground colour. See the
section "Draw Shapes and
Lines" for more on the Pencil
tool.*

 *The Impressionist Brush (▨)
creates artistic effects by
blending existing colours in
an image together. The
Impressionist Brush does not
add any foreground or
background colour to your
image. You can select the tool
from the menu that appears
when you right-click on the
Brush tool (▨).*

CHANGE BRUSH STYLES

You can select from a variety of predefined brush styles in Photoshop Elements to apply colour to your image in different ways. You can also create a custom brush style by specifying spacing, fade and other characteristics for your brush.

Select From a Predefined Set

1. In the Editor, click the **Brush** tool (▨).

2. Click the **Brush** ▪.

3. Click here to choose a set of brushes.

The set appears in the Brushes palette.

4. Click a brush style to select it.

The mouse pointer changes to the new brush shape.

Note: You can change the brush size.

5. Click here to choose a colour to apply with the brush. The actual colour applied may vary depending on the brush type.

6. Click and drag the brush on the photo.

Photoshop Elements applies the brush to the area.

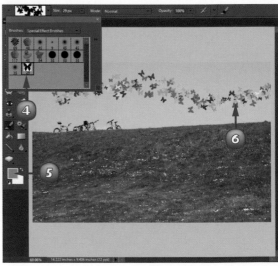

Customise a Brush

1 Click **Show Options** (▨).

A panel of brush options appears.

2 Click and drag the sliders (▥) or type values to define the new brush attributes.

A *You can limit the length of your brushstrokes with the Fade slider.*

B *You can randomise the painted colour with the Hue Jitter slider.*

C *You can change the shape of the brush tip by clicking and dragging here.*

You can also type values for the fade, the hue jitter and the shape of the brush tip.

D *The brush style appears in the Brushes menu.*

3 Click and drag the brush on the photo.

Photoshop Elements applies the customised brush to the area.

Apply Dots with a Brush

1 Click the **Show Options** button (▨) to open the brush settings.

2 Click and drag the Spacing slider (▥) to increase the value to greater than 100%.

When you click and drag a brush shape, you get dots or patches instead of a contiguous line.

ADD COLOUR WITH THE PAINT BUCKET TOOL

The Paint Bucket tool lets you fill areas in your image with solid colour. You can use this technique to change the colour of clothes, the sky, backgrounds and more. By default, when you apply the Paint Bucket tool, it affects adjacent pixels in the image. You can set the Paint Bucket's tolerance value to determine the range of colours the paint bucket affects when you apply it.

Select the Paint Bucket Tool

1. In the Editor, click the **Paint Bucket** tool (![icon]).

2. Click the **Foreground Color** box (■) to select a colour for painting.

Note: *For more, see the section "Set the Foreground and Background Colours."*

Set the Tolerance

3. Type a tolerance value from 0 to 255.

   Tolerance is the amount by which neighbouring pixels can differ from the selected pixel and still be affected.

   To paint over a narrow range of colours, type a small value; to paint over a wide range of colours, type a large value.

4. Click inside the image.

   Photoshop Elements fills an area of the image with the foreground colour.

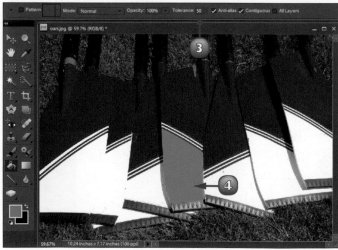

Set Image Opacity

5 To fill an area with semi-transparent colour, type a value of less than 100% in the opacity field.

6 Click inside the image.

Photoshop Elements fills an area with see-through paint.

Fill Noncontiguous areas

7 To fill noncontiguous but similar areas throughout the image, deselect the **Contiguous** check box (☑ changes to ■).

8 Click inside the selection.

Photoshop Elements fills similar areas of the image, even if they are not contiguous with the clicked pixel.

Reset a Tool to Default Settings

1 Click the tool you want to select in the Toolbox.

2 Click **Reset** (■) on the far left of the Options bar.

3 Click **Reset Tool** from the menu that appears.

A *You can click **Reset All Tools** from the menu to reset all the Photoshop Elements tools to their default settings.*

REPLACE A COLOUR WITH A BRUSH

You can replace colours in your image with the current foreground colour by using the Color Replacement tool. This gives you a free-form way of recolouring objects in your image while keeping the shading on the objects intact.

1 In the Editor, right-click on the **Brush** tool (■).

2 From the list that appears, click the **Color Replacement** tool (■).

3 Click the **Foreground Color** box to select a colour for painting.

4 Click here to choose a brush size and type.

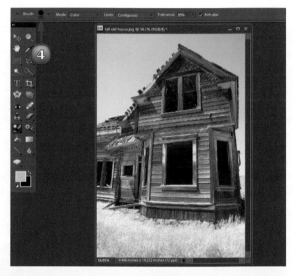

5 Type a tolerance value from 1% to 100%.

The greater the tolerance, the greater the range of colours the tool replaces.

6 Click and drag in your image.

Photoshop Elements replaces the colour.

 You can fill a selection with a solid or semi-transparent colour. Make a selection with a selection tool. Click Edit, Fill Selection. Select the colour you want to fill with and then set an opacity for the fill colour. Click OK.

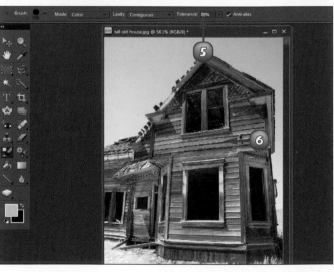

ADJUST COLOURS WITH THE SMART BRUSH

You can simultaneously select objects in your photo and apply colour adjustments to them with the Smart Brush tool. Different tool options enable you to increase, decrease, remove or transform colour in the objects.

1 In the Editor, click the **Smart Brush** tool (🖌).

    A *The Smart Paint menu opens.*

2 Click here to choose a category.

    Photoshop Elements lists the painting effects in that category.

3 Click an effect.

4 Press Enter to close the Smart Paint menu.

5 Click here to choose a brush style and size.

6 Click and drag over objects in your image to apply the tool.

    B *The effect is stored as a new adjustment layer.*

    C *You can click **Inverse** to invert your selection and apply the effect to the other pixels in your image.*

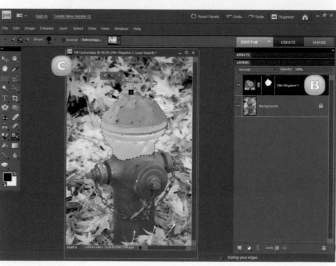

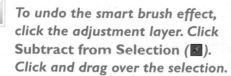

To undo the smart brush effect, click the adjustment layer. Click Subtract from Selection (◨). Click and drag over the selection.

CHAPTER 9 PAINTING AND DRAWING ON PHOTOS

DRAW SHAPES AND LINES

You can create solid shapes or lines in your image by using the many shape tools in Photoshop Elements. Shapes offer an easy way to add whimsical objects, labels or buttons to an image. You can customise the line with arrows, giving you an easy way to point out elements in your image.

When you add a shape or line to an image, Photoshop Elements places it in its own layer. This makes it easy to move and transform later on. Because shape and line objects are vector graphics in Photoshop Elements, they can be resized without a loss in quality.

Draw a Shape

1. In the Editor, right-click the **Rectangle** tool (■).

2. Click the **Custom Shape** tool (♥).

3. Click here to open the Custom Shapes menu.

4. Click a shape and press Enter to close the menu.

5. Click here to choose a colour for your shape.

   A. *You can click here to select a style, such as a 3-D style, for your shape.*

6. Click and drag your mouse pointer (+) to draw the shape.

   B. *Photoshop Elements places the shape in its own layer.*

   You can click and drag multiple times to create more than one shape.

 You can resize a shape by clicking Image, Transform Shape and selecting a transform command.

156

Draw a Line

1. In the Editor, right-click on the **Rectangle** tool (■).

2. Click the **Line** tool (◼).

3. Click here and then click **Start** or **End** to include arrowheads on your line (■ changes to ✓).

   Ⓐ *You can also specify the shape of the arrowheads by typing values here.*

4. Press **Enter** to close the menu.

5. Type a line weight.

6. Click here to choose a different line colour.

7. Click and drag your mouse pointer (+) to draw the line.

   Ⓑ *Photoshop Elements places the line in its own layer.*

ERASE AN AREA

You can use the Eraser tool to erase unwanted areas of your photo. When you apply the Eraser tool in the Background layer, the erased pixels are replaced with the current background colour. When you erase in other layers, the Eraser tool turns the pixels transparent, revealing any underlying layers.

1. In the Editor, click the **Eraser** tool (▣).

2. Click the **Background Color** box (□) to choose a colour to appear in place of the erased pixels.

Note: *For more, see the section "Set the Foreground and Background Colours."*

3. Click here to choose an eraser size and type.

   Ⓐ *You can also click here and adjust a slider to set an eraser size.*

Erase the Background Layer

④ Click the Background layer.

⑤ Click and drag the mouse pointer (○) to erase.

Portions of the Background layer are erased and filled with the background colour.

Erase a Normal Layer

⑥ Click a normal layer.

⑦ Click and drag the mouse pointer (○) to erase.

Portions of the layer are erased to reveal the underlying layer.

159

 You can right-click on the Eraser tool (⬛) to access other eraser types. You can use the Background Eraser tool (⬛) to sample a colour in your image and erase only that colour as you drag the tool over your image. The Magic Eraser tool (⬛) erases all the adjacent, similarly coloured pixels when you click it.

 In the Options bar, you can choose from three eraser modes: Brush, Pencil and Block. The default, Brush mode, enables you to apply the eraser to your image in a similar way to the Brush tool. Pencil mode acts like the Pencil tool while erasing, with the strokes having a harder edge. Block mode turns the eraser mouse pointer into a hard-edged square shape for erasing.

APPLY A GRADIENT

You can apply a *gradient*, which is a blend from one colour to another, to give objects in your image a radiant or 3-D look. You can apply a gradient to a selected portion of an image or the entire image.

1 In the Editor, make a selection.

   If you do not make a selection, the gradient is applied to the entire image.

2 Click the **Gradient** tool (▇).

   Ⓐ *A linear gradient (▇) is the default. You can select different geometries in the Options bar.*

3 Click the gradient swatch.

   The Gradient Editor dialog box opens.

4 Click a preset gradient type from the top box.

   Ⓑ *You can define a custom gradient by changing these settings.*

5 Click **OK**.

6 Click and drag the mouse pointer (✛) inside the selection to define the direction and transition of the gradient.

Dragging a long line with the tool produces a gradual transition.

Dragging a short line with the tool produces an abrupt transition.

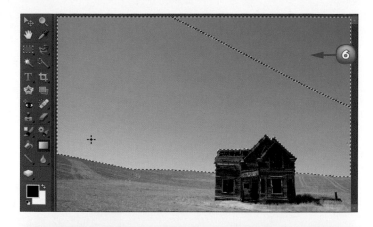

Photoshop Elements generates a gradient inside the selection.

Highlight an Object

1 Place the object in its own layer.

2 Create a new layer below the object and then select the new layer.

3 Click the **Gradient** tool (■).

4 Click the **Radial Gradient** button (■).

5 Click and drag the mouse pointer (✛) from the centre of the object outward to create the gradient.

161

CONTENTS

10

APPLYING FILTERS

You can use the filters in Photoshop Elements to quickly and easily apply enhancements to your image, including artistic effects, texture effects and distortions. Filters can help you correct defects in your images or let you turn a photograph into something resembling an impressionist painting. This chapter highlights a few of the more than 100 filters available in Photoshop Elements. For more on all the filters, see the Help documentation.

BLUR AN IMAGE

You can use the Blur filters to apply a variety of blurring effects to your photos. For example, you can use the Gaussian Blur filter to obscure background objects while keeping foreground objects in focus.

Blurring a busy background makes an image look as if it has a short depth of field. A short depth of field keeps the foreground subject in focus while placing the background out of focus.

1 In the Editor, select a layer.

   In this example, the scenery around the flower is selected.

2 Click **Filter**.

3 Click **Blur** and **Gaussian Blur**.

4 Click the minus (⬛) or plus (⬛) to zoom out or in.

5 Click the **Preview** check box (⬛ changes to ☑) to preview the effect in the image window.

6 Click and drag the **Radius** slider (⬛) to control the amount of blur.

7 Click **OK**.

Photoshop Elements applies the filter.

DISTORT AN IMAGE

You can use any of the Distort filters to stretch and squeeze your image, creating the appearance of waves, glass, swirls and more. For example, the Twirl filter turns the image into a swirl of colours and the Ripple filter adds wavelike effects.

To apply the filter to just part of your image, select that portion by using a selection tool.

① In the Editor, select the layer to which you want to apply a filter.

② Click **Filter**.

③ Click **Distort**.

④ Click a filter.

The filter's dialog box opens.

⑤ Make adjustments to the filter's settings to fine-tune the effect.

⑥ Click **OK**.

Photoshop Elements applies the filter.

In these examples, the Twirl and Ripple distortion filters are applied.

 Photoshop Elements has 106 filters grouped into 14 categories. Two of the more popular filters are Unsharp Mask (used for sharpening an image's focus, see Chapter 6) and Lighting Effects (which creates the illusion of highlights and other specialised lights in your photos, see Chapter 7).

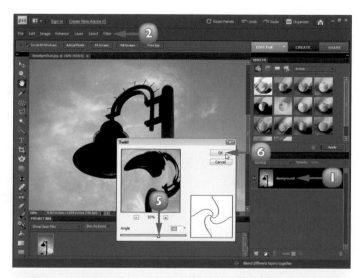

TURN AN IMAGE INTO A PAINTING OR SKETCH

You can use many of the Artistic filters in Photoshop Elements to make your image look as if you created it with a paintbrush or other art media. The Watercolor filter, for example, applies a painted effect by converting similarly coloured areas in your image to solid colours.

The Sketch filters add outlining effects to your image. The Charcoal filter, for example, makes an image look as if you sketched it in charcoal. The foreground is the charcoal colour and the background is the paper colour. Changing these colours alters the filter's effect.

To apply the filter to just part of your image, select that portion by using a selection tool.

1 In the Editor, select the layer to which you want to apply a filter.

In this example, the image has a single Background layer.

2 Click **Filter**.

Turn an Image into a Painting

3 Click **Artistic**.

4 Click a filter, in this case Dry Brush.

The Filter Gallery dialog box opens, displaying a preview of the filter's effect.

5 Adjust the filter's settings to fine-tune the effect.

A *With some filters, you can preview the effect before applying it to the image. Click the minus (□) or plus (⊞) signs to zoom out or in.*

B *You can select a different filter by clicking ▾.*

6 Click **OK**.

Photoshop Elements applies the filter.

Turn an Image into a Sketch

③ Click **Sketch**.

④ Click **Charcoal**.

The Filter Gallery dialog box opens, displaying a preview of the filter's effect.

⑤ Click and drag the sliders () to control the filter's effect.

⑥ Click **OK**.

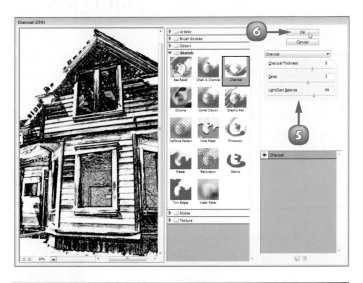

Photoshop Elements applies the filter.

In this example, the thickness of the charcoal strokes increases and the detail decreases.

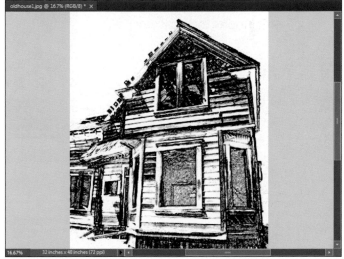

The Photocopy filter converts your image's shadows and midtones to the foreground colour and converts highlights to the background colour to make the image look like a photocopy.

APPLY MULTIPLE FILTERS

You can apply more than one filter to an image by using the Filter Gallery interface. It enables you to preview a variety of filter effects and apply them in combination.

Many filters open the Filter Gallery interface when you apply them. Not all the effects listed under the Photoshop Elements Filter menu appear in the Filter Gallery. Those not shown can be accessed in the Filter menu.

① In the Editor, select the layer to which you want to apply the filters.

In this example, the image has a single Background layer.

② Click **Filter**.

③ Click **Filter Gallery**.

The Filter Gallery dialog box opens, with the most recently applied filter selected.

The left pane displays a preview of the filtered image.

④ Click an arrow to display filters from a category (▶ changes to ▼).

⑤ Click a thumbnail to apply a filter.

Ⓐ *The filter appears in the filter list.*

6 Click the **New Effect Layer** button ().

B *The new effect appears in the filter list.*

You can click and drag effects in the list to change their order and change the look of your image.

7 Click a different triangle to display filters from another category.

8 Click a thumbnail to apply another filter.

You can repeat steps **6** to **8** to apply additional filters.

9 Click **OK**.

Photoshop Elements applies the filters.

✓ *You can apply filters to a type layer in your image, but you must first simplify the layer. Simplifying converts a type layer to a regular Photoshop Elements layer that you can no longer edit with the type tools.*

CONTENTS

ADDING TEXT ELEMENTS

Do you want to add letters and words to your photos and illustrations? Photoshop Elements lets you add text to your images and precisely control the appearance and layout of text. You can also stylise your text by using effects and other tools in Photoshop Elements.

ADD TEXT

Adding text enables you to label elements in your image or use letters and words in artistic ways. When you add text, it appears in its own layer. You can manipulate text layers in your image to move or stylise text.

Photoshop Elements comes with a number of expensive typefaces that are not typically preinstalled on computers.

1 In the Editor, click the **Horizontal Type** tool (T).

2 Click in the image where you want the text to begin.

3 Select a font, style and size for your text from these menus.

4 Click the **Color** .

5 Click a colour for your text.

When you position your mouse pointer ( ) over a colour, it changes to an eyedropper ( ).

6 Type your text.

To create a line break, press Enter.

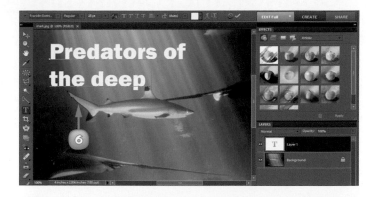

7 When you finish typing your text, click or press Enter on your keyboard's number pad.

A *You can click* *or press* Esc *to cancel.*

B *Photoshop Elements places the text in its own layer.*

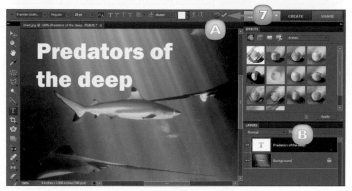

✓ **You can move the layer that contains the text. Click the layer of text, click the Move tool (⊕) and then click and drag to reposition your text.**

✓ **To add vertical text, right-click on the Horizontal Type tool (T) and then click the Vertical Type tool (T). You can also click the Vertical Type tool on the Options bar. Your text appears with a vertical orientation and lines are added from right to left. You can change the orientation of existing text in your image by selecting a text layer and then clicking the Change the Text Orientation button (T). This converts horizontal text to vertical text and vice versa.**

CHANGE THE FORMATTING OF TEXT

You can change the font, style, size and other characteristics of your text. This can help emphasise or de-emphasise your text.

1. In the Editor, click the **Horizontal Type** tool (T).

2. Click the text layer that you want to edit.

3. Click and drag to select some text from the selected layer.

   Ⓐ *You can double-click the layer thumbnail to select all the text.*

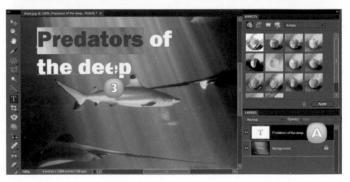

④ Click here to choose a font.

⑤ Click here to choose the text's style.

⑥ Click here to choose the text's size.

⑦ Click the **Anti-Aliased** button () to control the text's anti-aliasing.

⑧ When you finish formatting your text, click ✔ or press Enter on your keyboard's number pad.

Ⓑ *You can click ✖ or press Esc to cancel.*

Photoshop Elements applies the formatting to your text.

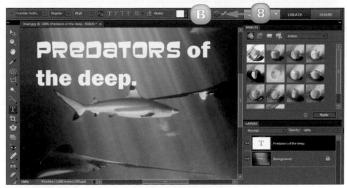

✓ **Anti-aliasing *is the process of adding semi-transparent pixels to curved edges in digital images to make the edges appear smoother. Text that you do not anti-alias can sometimes look jagged. You can control the presence and style of your text's anti-aliasing with the Options bar. At very small text sizes, anti-aliasing can be counterproductive and cause blurring.***

✓ ***When creating your text, click one of the three alignment buttons in the Photoshop Elements Options bar: Left Align Text (▤), Center Text (▤) or Right Align Text (▤). You may find these options useful when you create multi-line passages of text.***

CHANGE THE COLOUR OF TEXT

You can change the colour of your text to make it blend or contrast with the rest of the image. You can change the colour of all or just part of your text.

1 In the Editor, click the **Horizontal Type** tool (🅣).

2 Click the text layer that you want to edit.

3 Click and drag to highlight some text.

A *You can double-click the layer thumbnail to highlight all the text.*

④ Click here to choose a colour.

When you position your mouse pointer (🖑) over a colour, it changes to an eyedropper (🖋).

B *You can click here to open the Select Color dialog box.*

C *You can click **More Colors** to open the Color Picker for more colour options.*

⑤ Press Enter on your keyboard's number pad to close the colour menu.

⑥ Click ☑ or press Enter on your keyboard's number pad.

D *You can click ▧ or press Esc to cancel.*

Photoshop Elements changes the text to the new colour.

Use the Color Swatches Panel

① Click **Window** and then **Color Swatches** to open the panel.

② Click the text layer in the Layers panel.

③ Click and drag in the image window to highlight the text you want to recolour.

④ Click a colour in the Color Swatches panel.

The text changes colour. To see the actual new colour, click away from the type in the image window to deselect it.

CREATE WARPED TEXT

You can easily bend and distort layers of text by using the Warped Text feature in Photoshop Elements. This can help you stylise your text to match the theme of your image.

1. In the Editor, click the **Horizontal Type** tool (T).

2. Click the text layer that you want to warp.

3. Click the **Create Warped Text** button (T).

The Warp Text dialog box opens.

4. Click here to choose a warp style.

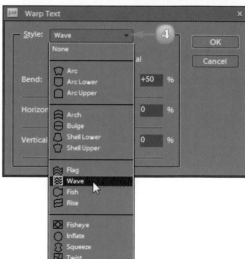

5 Click a radio button to select an orientation for the warp effect.

6 Adjust the Bend and Distortion values by clicking and dragging the sliders ().

You can also type Bend and Distortion values. A value of 0% means Photoshop Elements does not apply that aspect of a warp.

7 Click **OK**.

Photoshop Elements warps the text.

You can still edit the format, colour and other characteristics of the type after applying a warp.

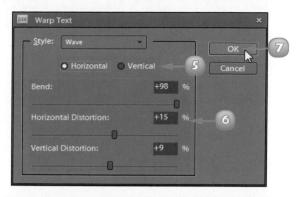

To unwarp text, click the Style
▇ in the Warp Text dialog box.
Click None. Click OK.

CREATE BEVELLED TEXT

You can give your text a raised look by adding a bevelled effect. Photoshop Elements offers several bevelled options in the Effects panel.

1 In the Layers panel, click a text layer.

2 In the Effects panel, click the **Layer Styles** button (▤).

3 Click here and then choose **Bevels**.

Photoshop Elements displays the bevel effects.

4 Click a bevel effect.

5 Click **Apply**.

Photoshop Elements applies the bevelling to the text.

A Photoshop Elements adds an icon (▤) to the layer to show that the layer includes an effect. You can double-click the icon to edit the effect.

ADD A SHADOW TO TEXT

You can cast a shadow behind your text to give the letters a 3-D look. Photoshop Elements offers several shadow options in the Effects panel.

① In the Layers panel, click a text layer.

② In the Effects panel, click the **Layer Styles** button (▣).

③ Click here to choose **Drop Shadows**.

Photoshop Elements displays the Drop Shadows effects.

④ Click a shadow effect.

⑤ Click **Apply**.

Photoshop Elements applies the shadow to the text.

Ⓐ *Photoshop Elements adds an icon (▣) to the layer to show that the layer includes an effect. You can double-click the icon to edit the effect.*

CONTENTS

12

APPLYING STYLES AND EFFECTS

You can apply special effects to your images by using the built-in styles and effects in Photoshop Elements. The effects let you add shadows, glows and a 3-D appearance to your art. You can also add special effects to your layers with layer styles.

FRAME A PHOTO WITH A DROP SHADOW

You can apply a drop shadow to make your photo look like it is floating above the image canvas.

You can also apply a drop shadow to a specific layer (see the section "Add a Drop Shadow to a Layer"). To add shadowing to text, see Chapter 11.

1. In the Editor, open the Effects panel.

2. Click the **Photo Effects** button (■).

3. Click here and then choose **Frame**.

   The Frame effects appear.

4. Double-click the **Drop Shadow Frame** effect.

A *Photoshop Elements duplicates the selected layer, adds extra space around the photo and then applies the effect.*

B *Photoshop Elements applies the drop shadow over a canvas with the current background colour, which is white in this example.*

Change the Colour of a Drop Shadow

1 After applying the drop shadow style, double-click the **Style** icon (■) to open the Style Settings dialog box.

2 Click here to open the Select Shadow Color dialog box.

3 Click **OK**.

A *Photoshop Elements changes the shadow colour.*

ADD A DROP SHADOW TO A LAYER

You can add a drop shadow to a layer to give objects in your photo a 3-D look. Style settings enable you to control the shadow's placement.

① In the Editor, open the Layers panel.

② Open the Effects panel.

③ Click the **Layer Styles** button (▣).

④ Click the layer to which you want to add a drop shadow.

⑤ Click here to choose **Drop Shadows**.

The Drop Shadow styles appear.

⑥ Click a drop shadow style.

⑦ Click **Apply**.

Photoshop Elements applies the drop shadow to the layer.

⑧ Double-click the **Style** icon (▨) in the affected layer.

The Style Settings dialog box opens.

⑨ Click and drag the **Lighting Angle** dial to specify the direction of the shadowing.

You can also type in an angle.

⑩ Click and drag the **Distance** slider (▮) to increase or decrease the distance of the shadow from your layer.

You can also type a distance.

⑪ Click **OK**.

Photoshop Elements applies the style settings.

Add Colour Shading to a Layer

① Click a layer.

② Open the Effects panel.

③ Click the **Layer Styles** button (▦).

④ Click here and then choose **Photographic Effects**.

⑤ Double-click an effect.

Photoshop Elements applies the shading.

CREATE A VINTAGE PHOTO

You can apply an effect that removes colour and adds a wrinkled texture to your photo, creating the look of an older snapshot.

① In the Editor, open the Effects panel.

② Click the **Photo Effects** button (▣).

③ Click here and then choose **Vintage Photo**.

An Old Paper effect appears.

④ Double-click the Old Paper effect.

A *Photoshop Elements duplicates the selected layer and then applies the effect.*

B *You can reduce the opacity of the new layer to make the effect more subtle.*

You can add the vintage effect to just part of your photo by making a selection before applying the effect.

ADD A FANCY BACKGROUND

You can add a fancy background to your image by using one of several colour or texture effects available in Photoshop Elements.

1 In the Editor, open the Layers panel.

2 Open the Effects panel.

3 Click the **Layer Styles** button (▣).

4 Click the layer to which you want to add the fancy background.

5 Click here and then choose **Patterns**.

The Pattern styles appear.

6 Double-click a style.

If you selected the Background layer in step **4**, a dialog box opens, asking if you want to make your background a normal layer.

7 Click **OK** and then click **OK** again in the dialog box that follows.

Photoshop Elements applies a pattern to the selected layer, creating a background behind the other layers.

 Where the effect is applied to a duplicate layer, you can reduce the opacity of the new layer to lessen the effect. Reducing the opacity to less than 100% allows the original content underneath to show through.

 Clicking ▣ in the Effects panel opens a menu that allows you to tailor the Effects panel to your liking. You can select different thumbnail sizes for each effect and display the names of the effects. Selecting Styles and Effects Help opens a Web browser with information about the different effects.

CONTENTS

13

SAVING AND SHARING YOUR WORK

Photoshop Elements lets you save your images in different file formats for use on the Web and in other applications. You can also share your photos by printing them.

You can use photos that you have edited in Photoshop Elements in a variety of creative projects. Some of the projects, such as the greeting card and the photo collage, can be output on your printer.

This chapter introduces you to some of the more interesting creative projects in Photoshop Elements.

SAVE AN IMAGE FOR THE WEB

You can save a file in a format suitable for publication on the Web.

The JPEG – Joint Photographic Experts Group – format is the preferred Web format for images. Photoshop Elements saves JPEG images at 72 dpi. GIF – Graphics Interchange Format – files are good for saving illustrations that have a lot of solid colour. The format supports a maximum of 256 colours. Photoshop Elements saves GIF images at 72 dpi. Unlike JPEG images, GIF images can include transparency.

PNG format, devised as a high-quality alternative to GIF and JPEG, can support more than 256 colours. However, it is not supported by all Web browsers.

1 In the Editor, click **File**.

2 Click **Save for Web**.

The Save For Web dialog box opens. Your original image appears on the left and a preview of the Web version is on the right.

Save a JPEG

1 Click here to choose **JPEG**.

2 Click here to choose a quality setting.

A *You can select a numeric quality setting from 0 (low quality) to 100 (high quality).*

The higher the quality, the larger the resulting file size.

3 Use the preview area to verify that the file quality and size are acceptable.

B *You can resize the image by typing dimensions or a percentage and then clicking* **Apply**.

4 Click **OK**.

The Save Optimized As dialog box opens.

5 Click here to choose a folder in which to save the file.

6 Type a file name. Photoshop Elements automatically assigns a .jpg extension if you do not specify an extension.

7 Click **Save**.

The original image file remains open.

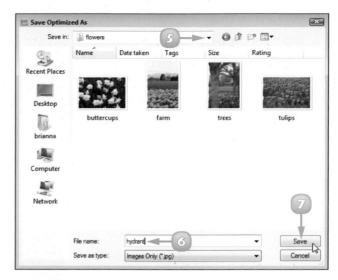

Save a GIF or PNG file

1 In the Save For Web dialog box, click here to choose **GIF, PNG-8 or PNG-24**.

Note: *The 24-bit PNG format gives a wider range of colours and better image quality but generally results in a larger file size.*

2 Click here to choose the number of colours (up to 256) to include in the GIF image.

(A) *You can resize the image by typing dimensions or a percentage and then clicking Apply.*

(B) *Click the Transparency check box (changes to) to ensure that any transparent areas remain transparent in the GIF or PNG image.*

3 Click **OK**.

4 In the Save Optimized As dialog box, choose a folder and type a file name.

5 Click **Save**.

CREATE A SLIDE SHOW

You can use the Create feature in Organizer to make a variety of projects by using the photos in your Organizer catalogue. For example, you can create slide shows and share them with others or turn your photos into album pages, calendars and even Web galleries.

Slide shows are easy to share with others by copying the finished file onto a disk or e-mailing it.

① In the Organizer, hold **Ctrl** and click the images you want to put in your slide show.

② Click **Create**.

③ Click **Slide Show**.

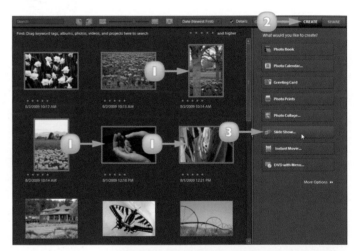

The Slide Show Preferences dialog box opens.

④ Choose a duration, transition and other options.

⑤ Specify the quality of the preview photos. Choosing a lower quality results in a smaller file size.

⑥ Click **OK**.

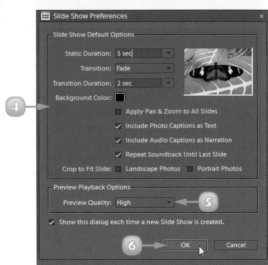

The Slide Show Editor dialog box opens.

Ⓐ To add more photos to your slide show, you can click **Add Media**.

Ⓑ Photoshop Elements displays thumbnails for the slides and icons for the transitions along the bottom of the Slide Show Editor.

Add Text to a Slide

① Click the slide to which you want to add text.

② Click **Add Text**.

The Edit Text dialog box opens.

③ Type your text.

④ Click **OK**.

Photoshop Elements adds the text to the selected slide.

The text properties appear.

⑤ Click and drag inside the text to position it.

⑥ Choose formatting options for your text.

✓ *In the Slide Show Editor dialog box, you can click and drag the thumbnails at the bottom to change their order in the slide show. To remove a slide entirely, right-click on it and then choose Delete Slide. If you have a lot of slides, you can click Quick Reorder to view and rearrange them in a larger window.*

✓ *To add music or narration to a slide show, click Add Media and then choose one of the audio options. You can also click the audio timeline below the slide and transition thumbnails. You can add an audio file that plays in the background while the slide show runs.*

continued ➡

197

CREATE A SLIDE SHOW *(continued)*

You can add clip art to a slide and create a title page for the slide show. You can control transition effects (how one slide flows to the next) and slide duration as well as set the show to loop continuously.

Organizer saves your slide show as either a WMV file or a PDF file. You can view WMV files with Windows Media Player. You can view PDFs with a variety of applications, including the free Adobe Reader.

Add Clip Art to a Slide

1. If the Extras panel is closed, click **Extras** to open it.

2. Click the slide to which you want to add clip art.

3. Click and drag the clip art to the slide.

   You can click and drag the clip art to reposition it.

   A. *Choose options here to resize or recolour the clip art.*

Change Transition Slides

1. Click a transition icon.

2. Click to choose a transition duration.

3. Click to choose a transition style.

4. Click the **Play** button (▶) to preview your slide show (▶ changes to Pause, ▮▮).

   A. *You can click **Full Screen Preview** to preview the slide show at maximum size.*

Add a Title Page to a Slide Show

1. Click a slide thumbnail. Your title page will be inserted after this slide.

2. Click **Add Blank Slide**.

   Ⓐ *Photoshop Elements adds a blank slide to your slide show.*

3. Click **Add Text**.

4. In the dialog box that opens, type a title for your page.

5. Click **OK**.

   You can click and drag the new title page to reposition it (for example, before the first slide in your slide show).

Save a Slide Show

1. Click **Save Project**.

   A dialog box opens, asking you to name your slide show.

2. Type a name.

3. Click **Save**.

   Photoshop Elements saves your slide show to the Organizer.

   Ⓐ *You can click **Output** to save the slide show as a PDF file or movie or burn it to a CD or DVD.*

4. Click here to close the Slide Show Editor and return to the Organizer.

CREATE A COLLAGE

Photoshop Elements lets you combine photos into a set of pages, which it calls a collage. You can customise the appearance of the photos and add artwork to the pages.

1. In the Organizer, hold **Ctrl** and click the images you want to include in your collage.

2. Click **Create**.

3. Click **Photo Collage**.

The Editor opens and displays your images in the Project Bin.

4. Click here to choose a page size for your collage.

   A. *You can choose a theme for your collage.*

5. Choose a layout for your collage.

   B. *Photoshop Elements displays a preview of the layout.*

6. Click **Done**.

Photoshop Elements creates a collage from the photos you selected.

To reposition your photo, click and drag inside it.

C To resize your photo, click and drag a corner handle.

D To crop your photo, click and drag a side handle.

⑦ Click the **Next** button (▶) to view and edit the next photo.

You can also click a page in the Project Bin to go directly to that page.

⑧ Click **File**.

⑨ Click **Save**.

The Save As dialog box opens.

⑩ Choose a destination folder.

⑪ Type a file name.

⑫ Click the **Include in the Organizer** check box (☐ changes to ☑) to add your collage to the Organizer.

⑬ Click **Save**.

Photoshop Elements saves your collage.

 You can add artwork to your collage by clicking and dragging items from the Content panel. After you complete step 6 above, Photoshop Elements opens the Content panel in the Panel Bin.

 The Photo Book feature enables you to design a custom book with one or more of your photos on each page. Similar to the collage, you can choose a theme and layout for the book pages. You can order a hard- or softcover version of the book through printing services such as Shutterfly and Kodak Gallery, or you can print book pages on your local printer. To start creating such a book from the Organizer, click the Create tab and then click Photo Book.

CREATE A GREETING CARD

You can design a printable greeting card by using one of your Photoshop Elements photos. Photoshop Elements lets you decorate your card with a variety of border styles and photo layouts. You can also add custom text.

A Photoshop Elements greeting card is more like a postcard than a foldable card. This feature creates a single image that you can print out.

1. In the Editor, open an image to use in your greeting card.

2. Click **Create**.

3. Click **Greeting Card**.

4. In the panel that appears, click **Print with Local Printer**.

   To order professionally printed cards, you can click the Shutterfly or Kodak Gallery buttons.

   The Greeting Card options appear.

5. Click here to choose a page size.

6. Choose a theme here.

   Ⓐ A pop-up preview of the theme appears.

7 Click here to scroll down and view the other options.

8 Click a layout option.

    B *A pop-up preview of the layout appears.*

9 Click the **Auto-Fill** check box to automatically add the open photo to your card (■ changes to ☑).

10 Click **Done**.

Photoshop Elements displays the greeting card in a new image window.

11 Click here and then choose **Text**.

12 Click a type style and drag it onto the greeting card.

13 Type your text and then press **Enter**.

14 In the bounding box, click and drag the handles to change the size of the text. You can click and drag inside the text to reposition it.

15 To save the greeting card, click **File** and then **Save**.

CREATE A FLIPBOOK

You can take a sequence of action photos and turn them into a flipbook, which is similar to a short movie. You can specify the frame rate of the movie as well as the dimensions.

① In the Organizer, hold **Ctrl** and click to select the photos you want to include in your flipbook.

② Click **Create**.

③ Click **More Options**.

④ Click **Flipbook**.

The Flipbook dialog box opens.

⑤ Type a playback speed between 1 and 30. *Fps* stands for frames per second.

Ⓐ *You can also click and drag the slider (■) to set a playback speed.*

Ⓑ *Your photos are ordered as they were in the Organizer. You can click the Reverse Order check box (■ changes to ✔) to reverse the order.*

6 Choose an output setting based on how the flipbook will be viewed. The setting determines the dimensions of the movie.

C *You can click* **Details** *for an explanation of the current setting.*

7 Click the **Play** button (▶) to preview your flipbook.

D *You can click and drag the slider (▮) to the left and right to cycle through the photos.*

E *You can click the* **Previous** *button (◀▮) to go to the previous photo.*

F *You can click the* **Next** *button (▮▶) to go to the next photo.*

G *You can deselect the* **Loop Preview** *check box (☑ changes to ▪) to stop the preview from looping.*

8 Click **Output**.

The Save dialog box opens.

9 Type a file name for your flipbook.

H *Only the Windows Media file type is supported.*

10 Click here to choose where to save the flipbook.

11 Click **Save**.

Photoshop Elements saves the flipbook.

The flipbook is also added to the Organizer.

PRINT A PHOTO

You can print your Photoshop Elements images to create hard copies of your work. You can then add your photos to a physical photo album.

1. Make sure the layers you want to print are visible.

Note: *An eye icon (👁) means that a layer is visible.*

This example shows printing from the Editor. You can also select an image and print from the Organizer.

2. Click **File**.

3. Click **Print**.

The Print dialog box opens.

4. Select your printer and paper settings. These will vary depending on the make and model of your printer.

5. Select a print type.

6. Select a print size. You can select from popular photo sizes or specify custom dimensions.

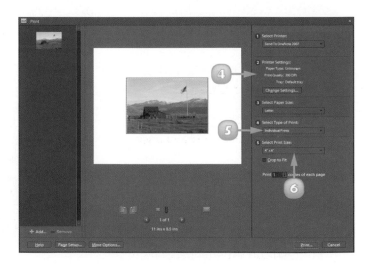

(A) *You can click and drag the slider (■) to zoom the photo.*

(B) *You can click here to rotate the photo.*

(C) *You can click and drag your photo within the print size boundary.*

(7) Type the number of copies to print.

(8) Click **Print**.

A smaller Print dialog box opens.

(D) *You can click Preferences to set printer-specific options.*

(9) Click **Print** to print the image.

Add Text to a Printed Photo

(1) In the Print dialog box, click **More Options**.

(2) Click **Printing Choices**.

(3) Click here to print a caption if your photo has one (■ changes to ☑).

(A) *You can click here to print the date the photo was taken or the file name.*

(B) *You can use these settings to print a solid border around the photo.*

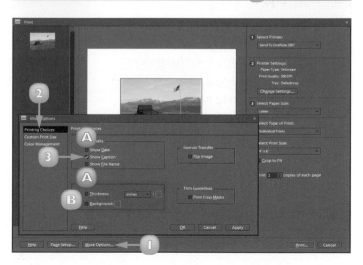

INDEX